How to ！
Based Food Business:

Turn Your Foodie Love into Serious Cash with a Food Business Startup

(The Work from Home Series: Book 3)

By

SAM KERNS

RainMaker Press

Books by Sam Kerns

How to Work from Home and Make Money: 10 Proven Home-Based Businesses You can Start Today (Work from Home Series: Book 1)

How to Build a Writing Empire in 30 Days or Less (Work from Home Series: Book 2)

How to Start a Home-Based Food Business: Turn Your Foodie Dreams into Serious Income with a Food Business Startup (Work from Home Series: Book 3)

How to Brand Your Home-Based Business: Why Business Branding is Crucial for Even the Smallest Startups (Work from Home Series: Book 4)

How to Quit Your Job Today and Become a Virtual Assistant (Work from Home Series: Book 5) Coming Spring 2017 (Sign up at RainMakerPress.com to receive advanced notice of its release.)

Thank you for buying

How to Start a Home-Based Food Business:
Turn Your Foodie Love into Serious Cash
with a Food Business Startup
(The Work from Home Series: Book 3)

Sign up at my website RainMakerPress.com
for special offers, promotions, and information
about new releases in this series.

Table of Contents

CHAPTER ONE:

Can I Really Sell Food
Made in My Own Kitchen?

D o your insides start jumping for joy when you see a perfectly frosted cupcake or cookie? Or do you love the look of taste of delicately scented violet lavender syrup or a mouthwatering strawberry and lime jam? Or are you more of a savory person and melt when you see a homemade canned jar of spicy salsa, beautifully packaged dried pasta, or seasoned nuts with just the right amount of spice?

If food excites you as much as it does me, you just might be a foodie. And in today's food-centered world, there is serious money to be made with your passion.

Food consumption has really changed in the past decade or so, and now more than ever, people want to know what's in their food, where it came from and who made it. That's bad news for businesses that mass produce food, but great news for those in the cottage food industry.

You see, in the past individuals who wanted to sell

1

food were required to involve the state health inspectors and lease commercial kitchens in order to sell directly to the public. Obviously, that prevented a lot of people from pursuing their food dreams. But over the past few years, many states have passed cottage food laws, and these special laws are designed to give home chefs and bakers the right to produce products from their homes and sell them to the public.

But as you can imagine, the laws are created by individual states, so each one is different. Some states, like Wyoming, have passed bills that give home-based food business owners wide latitude and allows them to sell both non-perishable foods and perishable ones like some cooked meats, casseroles, and soups. Most states only allow producers to sell non-perishable foods and have strict guidelines about what cottage food producers can and cannot sell. And one state—New Jersey—has yet to pass cottage food laws. Other states don't have cottage food laws on the books, but still allow home cooks to sell their products. But things are improving, and as more and more consumers demand foods that are baked by people they trust instead of mass corporations, new laws are constantly being introduced and existing ones updated and improved.

When you're ready to learn about the cottage laws in your state, I've included a state-by-state summary of all the current cottage laws in chapter ten of this book.

But there are some general guidelines that apply to most state's cottage laws. Here are some things that you might need to get started. (Again, be sure to check the guide for your state to be sure.)

- A business license
- A kitchen inspection

- A zoning permit
- A rule about pets. (Some states won't allow them in your home, others forbid them in the kitchen, while other states don't specify any rules about pets.)

In addition to these general rules, some states limit what home-based cooks can sell. The list of approved foods typically looks something like this:

- Baked goods like cupcakes, cookies, brownies, cakes, pies and breads.
- Some candy
- Canned items such as jams and pickles
- Dry nut mixes, cereals, granola, seeds, popcorn, or dry mixes for cakes and cookies.

When you sell food items from your home, the state also limits where you can sell them. For example, some state limit home cooks to selling at farmer's markets, while other states allow cottage food producers to sell their goods at:

- Farmer's markets
- Charity events
- Events run by non-profit organizations
- From your home
- Online
- Wholesale to restaurants or specialty shops

Unfortunately, some states—but not all—don't allow you to sell to restaurants, businesses, or to online buyers. (In these states, you can have a website to promote your business, but you can't sell your products to online customers.)

In addition to the limits on where you can sell, states set a limit on how much you can sell before you have to move up to the next step and rent a commercial kitchen. The limits vary wildly. For instance, in Wisconsin, you can only earn $5,000 per year and stay safely under the cottage food laws, but in Texas you can earn up to $50,000 per year. Be sure to check your state's guidelines.

Finally, each state requires that you place specific food labels on the products you sell. Some of the things you must list on your labels are the name of the person who prepared it, the address where it was made, the ingredients in the product, any food allergens present, and more. You'll find the label requirements for your state at the link to your state's cottage food laws in chapter ten.

So, that's the cottage laws summed up in a quick guide, but of course, the topic is much deeper and there's a lot to learn. The purpose of this book is to provide you with everything you'll need to start your own cottage food business in your state. I'll cover everything you need to know such as how to attend to the business aspects of your food company, how to brand your business to make customers want to buy your products and trust you as a cook, how to decide on a product and test market it, where to sell it and how to best approach the gate keepers at selling events, and more.

In addition, I've noticed that many books on this subject assume that most readers are already familiar with the basics, but I don't believe that's true. For instance, would you know how to transport a thousand cupcakes? Where to source ingredients in bulk in order to keep your operating costs down and increase your profits? How to keep your icing from melting in extreme heat while selling them at a market in summer? These are just some of the basic questions I'll address in this book.

In other words, this book will serve as a guide—a complete guide—to helping you get started in your own home-based food business.

So, are you ready to start on the path toward your foodie dreams? I'm excited to share my knowledge with you!

But First, Who am I to Write This Book?

If you've read my author bio, then you know that I'm a serial entrepreneur. I've opened and closed many businesses in my lifetime, and although I've enjoyed each type of the various businesses I've run, I have to admit that one of the things I love most about solopreneurship is the challenge. There is nothing I love more than taking an idea and turning it into a smoothly run, profitable business. And this book was born of that desire.

Let me explain.

I bake. There—it's out in the open. I'm a guy and I bake.

Can we please move on?

Specifically, I bake specialty brownies that are so good I've had local stores approach me and ask me to sell them wholesale so they can turn around and sell them to their customers. I get phone calls from friends begging me to bake a batch. Yeah, my brownies are that good.

So when I heard about the changes in the law allowing people to start home-based food businesses, my entrepreneurial mind starting spinning. I have a great product, so in my mind, there was no reason why I couldn't create a profitable business. I should just open one, right?

Fortunately, that's not the way I roll. I have never simply opened a business and learned as I go—instead I conduct so much research that I know absolutely everything there is to know before I begin. In other words, I leave no room for error. I want the information up front so I can make the best decisions and build a successful business.

Otherwise, what's the point?

So, when the idea of opening a cottage food business occurred to me, I began researching and I didn't stop for months. That's where this book comes in. There is a lot to know about this type of business, and one thing I learned is that there is simply nowhere that you can get all of the information in one place.

Until this book.

Don't believe me? Take a look at all the other books on the subject and just see if the author provided a state-by-state index of all the cottage food laws. Let me save you some time. They don't.

And recipes that fit into the guidelines of the laws? Nope, you won't find them in other books. How about serious insight into how to best brand, package and market your home-based food business? You'll only find that in this book.

So, let my obsessive research, along with my entrepreneurial skills, help you in your own business. I've done the hard work for you, so all you have do is follow the plan I've outlined in this book and you'll be on your way to building your very own food business. And all the newbie questions you have but are too embarrassed to ask? I had them, too and I've included the answers to them all in this book.

Oh, and the brownies? They're a hit. Hit me up at RainMakerPress.com and I'll let you know if you can find them in your area. (Unfortunately, I live in a state that doesn't allow me to sell them online.)

So, let's get started, shall we?

CHAPTER TWO:

Is a Food Business Right for You?

It's easy to imagine yourself surrounded by beautifully decorated cupcakes or chili and lime flavored almonds, but the truth is, the food business is about much more than making great food. Just as in any successful business endeavor, you'll need a thoughtful business plan in place before you begin, product ideas and recipes, carefully sought out sources for packaging and ingredients, a list of places where you can sell your product, a marketing plan, and of course, great tasting food that will have people buying from you again and again. (We'll cover all of this and more in later chapters.)

And here's the truth—not every great cook should start their own food business. What? I can hear the protests of some readers, but if there's one thing I am it's honest. Many, many home chefs have tried to take their products to the masses, and ended up with truckloads of food they couldn't sell. Why? Because they thought cooking mouthwatering food was the only requirement for success.

But it's not.

Let's be honest—solopreneurship is hard work. In addition to an ability to cook or bake products people will pay for, you'll also have to run a profitable business. So let's start out this book by busting some common myths and talk about the five types of people who should not start a home-based food business, or any business for that matter.

If you recognize yourself in this list, you'll either have to do some serious soul-searching and make significant changes, or resign yourself to making your fabulous foods for friends and family.

A Person Driven by Others

Ask any entrepreneur and they'll tell you that the number one trait needed for success is drive. But the key here is that the drive must come from you. Hearing from others how successful you might be if you sold your food to the public is one thing, but if it's what's driving you, trouble could lie ahead.

On the other hand, if you lie awake at night imaging your packaging ideas, or coming up with new recipes, you likely have the drive needed to make your food business a success.

A Person with no Cooking or Baking Experience

When people buy specialty food items, they expect the great tastes and experience that comes from eating food cooked or baked by an expert chef. Now that's not to say you can't develop your cooking skills and open a wildly successful food business. But until you've developed those skills, you should focus on practicing and honing the skills you need to make people say "Wow!" when they taste your product.

A Person Who Wants it Easy

If you've read my other books, then you probably already know what I'm going to say: running a successful business isn't for sissies. It isn't for those people who think they can only work when they want to, or want to run a business so they can have an expansive life outside of work. Now, I know that many other books feed you this enticing little lie, but the truth is that running a food business, or any type of business, is hard work.

Need a visual?

Imagine the night before you're scheduled to set up at a popular farmer's market. You may have to bake 500 cupcakes, 250 loaves of bread, or roast and season pounds and pounds of nuts. Then, after you've stayed up half the night baking or cooking and packaging your product, you'll have to transfer it all into your carrying containers and load it into your car. Or if the temperature is wrong, you'll have to do that about 5 am the next morning. Then, you'll have to rise early and haul everything to the site where you'll set it up. And for the next few hours, you'll have to be alert enough to mingle with customers, hand out samples, sell, make change, and answer all the questions you'll get about your product. And just when you think you can't take another step without falling asleep mid-stride, you'll have to pack up any products you didn't sell and haul them back home or to a donation site.

Whew! Needless to say, if you're thinking about

opening a food business because you want to take it easy, you might want to think again.

A Person with No Support

Running a food business is hard work, both physically and mentally. And in this type of business, unless you're a physically strong person, you'll need help moving the product, tables, and display units to and from your selling sites. Ideally, the person who helps you will be family or a friend so you won't need to pay them, which would dip into your precious early profits.

And in addition to physical help, you'll likely need some sort of emotional support, especially in the early months. If you have family or friends who will support you as you run your business, it will go a long way in keeping you sane as you build your business.

But what if you're alone and don't have either? I highly recommend that you develop some friendships even before you launch your business. A good place to start is at the sites where you'll be selling your product. For example, if you plan to sell your products at your local farmer's market, visit it frequently and befriend some of the vendors. Tell them that you're in the process of starting your own cottage food business, and ask them for advice. You'd be amazed at how many people will share insights and be a support for you as you begin.

A Person Who Doesn't Have (or Want to Learn) Business Know-How

Baking the perfect macaroon or lavender lemon jam is important, but if you're going to be successful as a business owner, you'll also need to attend to the business side of things. For example, before you decide how much to charge for your products, you'll need to create a cost sheet so you'll know exactly what it costs to make them. You'll also need to pay attention to booth fees wherever you set up, both sales tax as well as personal income tax, employee pay, packaging costs and a multitude of other things that will make or break your business.

Now I understand that not everyone is born understanding how to run a business, but if your dream is to work for yourself and start a food business, you'll need to learn how to run it. You can start by taking a couple of entrepreneur classes at your local college or an online course at places like Udemy.

But if you have even a base set of business skills, you'll know everything you need to about running a food business by the time you finish this book. It's my mission to not only teach you how to run this type of business, but also to give you the tools and business know how you'll need in order to make your business a success.

7 More Things to Consider

Okay, so you read all the warnings, and you're convinced that you have what it takes to start and run a successful cottage food business. Before we get to the next chapter and start building your business, let's take a look at seven more things you really should consider before taking the leap.

Your Kitchen Will Belong to the Business

Gone will be the days when the kitchen is a place to relax and cook dinner seven nights a week. On the days you're making product, the kitchen will be dedicated solely to your business. You may be okay with that, but will your family? After all, if you're baking 500 cupcakes for a sale the next day and your teenager wants to make a pot of macaroni and cheese, things could get dicey.

Where Will You Sell Your Products?

Remember that each state has different laws about where home-based food businesses can sell products, so you need to check chapter ten in the back of this book to determine where you're allowed to sell. Most states allow vendors to sell at farmer's markets, events sponsored by nonprofit organizations, charity events, from your home, and in some instances, small specialty shops, and online. For example, in Texas, cottage food producers aren't allowed to sell online or to third parties like retailers or restaurants, but California allows online sales, and if the vendor applies for a "Class B" license, they can also sell to third parties.

Depending on the product you plan to make, you may be able to sell from one or more of these location types. Do some serious thinking and determine where you think your potential customers are more likely to find you.

Who is Your Target Customer?

Next, you'll need to understand who your ideal buyer is. For instance, if you make cupcakes that are baked in ice cream cones and decorated in fun colors, your target audience is kids. You'll likely find them at fairs, school events, and birthday parties. You can contact the event coordinators at places where many kids will be in attendance and sell your cupcakes there, or you can market to moms who put on birthday parties and sell them out of your home.

Are You Allowed to Operate
a Home-Based Business?

Another thing you'll have to consider is whether or not you're legally allowed to operate a business out of your home. Each city and neighborhood has different zoning laws, and you'll need to determine if yours allows you to run a business from your home. The best way to determine this is to call your local zoning or planning department and ask. The IRS publishes a list on their website with links to all the state's government websites, and you should be able to find the right department there.

Do You Rent Your Home?

Finally, if you rent your home, you'll need to get permission from your landlord to run your business from their property. Approach them with the idea professionally and courteously, because if they don't agree, it could quickly put an end to your plans. It might help if you submit a written proposal telling them about your business, and explain how it will affect their property. For example, you may use the oven more than a traditional renter would, so you might offer to replace it when you move out.

Are you Innovative?

In order to stay competitive in the food business, you must constantly be innovative in your approach to food. There is just too much competition to rest on your accomplishments and take your success for granted. Newbies are arriving on the scene all the time, and they'll be excited to show off their newest creations. Whether you're selling fruit pies or spiced pickles, you should continue to experiment and find new ways to present your products.

How Big do You Want to Get?

Depending on your goals, you can contain your business to a small one person shop that only sells on weekends at the local famer's market, or you can go big and expand your business beyond cottage laws and venture into the land of commercial kitchens and nationwide distribution. The choice is entirely dependent on what you want from your business and how much work you're willing to put into it. The majority of this book is about home-based food businesses, but if after reading it you decide you want to go bigger, don't worry. I'll give you some direction and tips on how to take your business to the next level in chapter nine.

Are you still with me? If you are, then I'm sure you've got what it takes to become a cottage food producer and start earning an income doing what you love. Before we get to the fun stuff, we have one more thing to talk about: the administrative things you need to do to legally set up your home-based cottage food business.

The Seven Things You Must Do to Start a Cottage Food Business

Create a Business Plan

It can be tempting to skip this step, but if you want your food business to be successful, you'll have to create one. Fortunately, because you won't have to make a huge investment in this type of business, your plan doesn't need to be that complex. In fact, it's possible to create a 1 to 3 page business plan that will guide you and your business to success. One of the best plans I've seen is found at **bplans.com**, where you can download a free template to help you create your ideal plan.

Find Someone in the Business

In the cottage food business, there's one thing you can count on: things will never happen as you expect them to. You'll need someone to talk to when it rains on market day after you've been up all night baking cupcakes, or who can tell you where to find that unique canning set you want. Ideally, you'll find a mentor who is in the business, or is familiar with all aspects of it. Ask around at your local restaurant supply company or bakery wholesale shop for the names of people who would be willing to mentor newbies. You can also find support at the Cottage Food Association of America and the online community forums at Forrager.com.

In addition, you'll need a mentor to help you with the business side of things. You can find them at **score.org** where you'll be assigned a small business mentor free of charge.

Decide on the Legal Structure of Your Business

How you legally structure your business is important because it can protect you from personal consequences should your business get into debt or be sued by a customer. The majority of home-based businesses are set up as sole proprietorships, which means there is no legal line between you and your business. That means if your business goes into debt or gets sued, the debtors or court can take your personal assets. This is the easiest business structure to set up, and many home-based business owners use it.

You can create a legal line between you and your business by structuring your business as an LLC, which will protect your personal assets from lawsuits or insurance claims as long as it was an employee who caused the damage and not you. This type of business license is also easy to establish.

In order to completely protect your personal assets, you'll need to structure your business as a corporation, but in order to stay protected, you'll need to ensure that your personal accounts never mix with your business account. Entrepreneur.com puts out an in-depth overview of all your options, and I highly recommend that you read it.

Register Your Business Name

You'll need to register your business name with either your local county clerk's office or your state to ensure that no one else begins to use it. For example, if you build up a good custom cookie business using your business name, someone can come along and call their business the same thing unless your name is registered. In order to find your local county clerk's office, log onto the SBA's site where you'll find a chart which lists all government offices by state.

Register for State and Local Taxes

You'll not only have to pay federal income taxes, but also state and local taxes such as income tax, disability tax, and employment taxes. In addition, different states have different rules about which foods are charged sales tax. For instance, in Texas, I don't have to charge sales tax for my brownies if I don't provide a fork to the customer, but your state might be different. Use the same SBA **state-by-state list** of links to determine the requirements in your state.

Check the Zoning Laws in Your Neighborhood
Every city has zoning laws, and sometimes those laws can prevent entrepreneurs from working out of their houses, or at the minimum, hampering their efforts. For instance, if you want to open a cake decorating business and expect people to be in and out of your home choosing colors and designs, you'll first have to clear it with your zoning department. In addition, some cities don't allow cottage food businesses to put up signs or have excessive cooking odors coming from their homes, while other states like Texas don't allow zoning regulators to have any authority over cottage businesses.

There isn't a website I can direct you to for the information because every city, town and even neighborhood has different laws, so you'll have to get in touch with your local city planning office to learn about the rules in your area.

Get Your Cottage Food License
These rules also vary greatly state to state. Some states simply ask you to take a food handlers course online that costs about $7, while others require you to have a kitchen inspection, submit recipes, and put limitations on whether or not you can have pets in your home. You'll find a state-by-state list of the relevant rules in chapter ten of this book.

Buy Some Insurance
Finally, it's a good idea to purchase product liability insurance when you sell food to the public. This type of

insurance policy ensures that if someone gets sick from your food, has an allergic reaction, suffers from food contamination, or you experience damage to a rented property or have missing or damaged supplies, you won't have to pay the damages—the insurance company will. You can either talk to your local agent or use an industry expert like those at the Food Liability Insurance Program. (fliprogram.com) There, you can get a policy for $299 a year if your business earns $50,000 or less annually.

Now that we've gotten the practical things out of the way, let's have some fun. In the next chapter, we'll talk about the different foods you can make and the pros and cons of each one. I'll even give you a few recipe ideas that fall within the cottage food laws. Ready? Let's get to dreaming.

Food Business Secret Ingredient No. 1: Position Your Product Correctly

No matter how good your product is, if you don't position it correctly to consumers, it won't sell. This is true whether you sell to the masses at farmer's markets, to the business lunch crowd, from an online shop, or to mom's buying for their children's birthday parties. Justin Gold of Justin's Nut Butters learned this lesson the hard way. When he initially began selling the squeeze packs of his nut butters, he positioned them as "energy packs," and they didn't sell because people didn't know what to do with them. After store owners asked him to remove them from the shelves, he rethought the design and labeled them as peanut butter. Suddenly, they began flying off the shelves.

In your business, think about your products and make sure consumers understand their purpose and benefits. And remember, Justin started his business selling locally at a farmer's market!

CHAPTER THREE:

Food Ideas and Recipes for Every Palate

While it's true that home-based business owners can only produce what the state allows, that doesn't mean you don't have options. In fact, as long as you keep to your state's cottage law guidelines, your only limitation is your imagination. Now, having said that, I do realize that some states severely limit what people can make and sell, but even in those states, a little creativity can go a long way in helping you produce a unique product that people want to buy.

Sometimes people already know what to sell, and typically it's because:

- They have a family recipe that's been handed down over generations. For instance, that canned peach cobbler your great, great grandmother was famous for.

- They have a signature food that is always in demand. That pumpkin butter you make every year when the pumpkins are ripe? It would be a great thing to sell to the public.

- They love to combine great food and art. These are the cake decorators and cupcake makers who have a knack for making food look like a piece of art. They do well in all types of selling situations, from special events to private parties.

But if you're like many people, you're looking for ideas. You love to cook, and while you have a few general ideas, you haven't decided on one particular food. Relax. There are plenty to choose from. But before you read this rest of this chapter, I urge you skip to chapter ten and quickly read the cottage laws for your state. In them, you'll find out exactly which types of foods your state allows cottage food producers to sell.

After you understand the rules where you live, browse through the following pages and see if you can't get inspired. In them, I'll talk about some food product ideas and just because I'm a nice guy, I'll even throw in a few recipes. Happy browsing!

Sweets

Let's begin with the obvious. The great majority of home cooks decide to sell sweets such as cakes, cupcakes, pies, and other pastries. And the reason so many of them decide to go this route? Because they sell! Just think for a moment—every party you've ever attended had some sort of baked goods on offer. Whether it was a birthday party for a child or an adult, a wedding, a retirement party, a business celebration, or any other event you can think of, they all had sweets. And desert type baked goods sell in places other than parties. Farmer's markets, charity events, specialty shops, online stores, catering businesses, and expos all have vendors that set up and sell sweets.

But today's baked deserts are different than those that your grandmother used to make. Today, they not only taste good, but they're beautiful. I mean seriously, some of the cakes and cupcakes I've seen look like they belong in a museum! Just take a look at these beauties and tell me it wasn't an artist who made them.

If you think sweets might be the right product for you, take a look at this list and see if anything jumps out at you. (Most states don't allow you to sell anything that has to be refrigerated, which is why you won't see things like cream puffs and cheesecake on this list.)

- Cakes
- Pies
- Donuts
- Fried pies
- Brownies
- Cookies
- Macaroons
- Mini cakes
- Candy
- Fudge (that's been baked)
- Croissants
- Danishes
- Scones
- Peanut butter bars
- Whoopie pies
- Eclairs
- Cannoli
- Strudel
- Tarts
- Cobbler
- Cinnamon rolls
- Turnovers
- Fritters
- Streusel
- Rugelach

And the list goes on. Some of the pastries are just simple and plain, but taste fantastic. Others, like cupcakes and cakes should be elaborately decorated with delicious frosting and beautiful or whimsical decorations.

What most people don't know is that professional bakers typically only use a couple of basic cupcake recipes and alter then by using a variety of different frosting flavors. If you have a basic vanilla cupcake recipe and a chocolate one, you can make a vast assortment of flavors to please anyone.

For example, if you want a lemon cake, add some lemon extract or lemon peel to the vanilla recipe. If you want a rose cake, add rose extract. But whatever finished product you desire, you can start with this simple recipe that's been adapted from Life, Love, and Sugar.

One more thing—we'll get into the whys and how's of product testing later in the book, but always remember that each product you decide on should be thoroughly tested before taking it to market, and this recipe is no exception.

Moist and Fluffy Vanilla Cupcakes
Yields 28 cupcakes

Ingredients:
3 ⅓ cups all-purpose flour
2 cups sugar
½ tsp baking soda
½ tsp baking powder
1 ½ cups unsalted butter at room temperature
¼ tsp salt
3 egg whites
6 tsp vanilla extract
2 tsp almond extract
1 cup sour cream
1 cup milk

Directions:
1. Preheat your oven to 350 degrees F.
2. In a large mixing bowl, whisk together the sugar, flour, baking powder and baking soda
3. Add the butter, egg whites, vanilla extract, milk, and sour cream. Mix until smooth without over mixing.
4. Fill your cupcake liners with a scoop until they're just over half full.
5. Bake 18-20 minutes.
6. Cool the cupcakes for a couple of minutes, then place them on a cooling rack until completely cooled.

In addition to a vanilla recipe, you'll need a chocolate one. To make variations of it, you can add peanut butter, mint, nuts, or anything else your creative inner baker comes up with. Here's the basic recipe, also adapted from Life, Love, and Sugar.

Basic Chocolate Cupcakes
Yields 24 cupcakes

Ingredients:
2 cups flour
¾ cups Hershey's Special Dark Cocoa powder
2 tsp baking soda
1 tsp salt
2 large eggs
1 cup buttermilk
1 cup vegetable oil
1 ½ tsp vanilla extract
1 cup boiling water

Instructions:
1. Whisk together all the dry ingredients
2. Add the eggs, buttermilk and oil to the dry ingredients and mix them well.
3. Add the vanilla extract to the boiling water and add it to the mixture. Mix it well.
4. Using a scoop, put the batter into cupcake pans and bake at 300 degrees F for 20 to 25 minutes.
5. Allow cupcakes to cool completely when done.

Be sure to allow your cupcakes to cool completely before frosting them. If you're not going to use the cupcakes that day, it's okay to freeze them and wait to frost them until the day of your sale.

To freeze your cakes, wrap them each individually in plastic wrap, then put them in an airtight container or freezer bag. They will keep for a couple of days like this, and still be moist and airy when they thaw.

And to Top it Off

Of course, if you're selling cupcakes to the public, they have to be topped with delicious and beautiful frosting. And luckily, the same principal holds true for frosting: you only need a good basic recipe that you can adjust as your ideas and flavor profiles call for it.

Keep in mind that if you're going to sell outdoors at events like farmer's markets or fairs during warmer months, you won't be able to use straight butter in your buttercream recipe because the heat will cause the frosting to slide off the cupcake and create a mess—which is not good for sales.

One way to get around this potential disaster is to use half butter and half shortening. The shortening holds up better in the heat, and most customers will never taste the difference. Here's a great basic recipe you can adapt and add your own flavors to for different variations.

Butter and Shortening Frosting
Large batch

Ingredients:
1 cup salted butter
1 cup shortening
8 cups powdered sugar
3-6 tbsp water (or cream)
2 tsp vanilla extract

Directions:
1. Combine the shortening and butter.
Mix it until smooth.
2. Add 4 cups of the powdered sugar and again,
mix it until it's smooth.
3. Add the vanilla extract and 2-4 tbsp of water
or cream. Mix.
4. Add the rest of the powdered sugar and mix until
it's smooth. If necessary, add more liquid to reach
the right consistency.

An Icing That Withstands the Heat

Some of you are located in areas where a standard buttercream icing would never stand up to the extreme outside temperatures. (I'm talking to you Arizona and Texas!) Luckily, there is a tried and true recipe that bakers in those areas rely on to keep their cupcakes looking pretty, even when the heat is melting everything else outside. Here it is:

Indydebi's Crisco-Based Buttercream Icing

Ingredients
1 ⅓ cups Crisco
⅓ to ½ cup milk, depending on the
consistency you desire
3 tbsp powered dream whip (This powered whipped
toppingis made by Kraft and you can typically find it
in the cake or sugar isle of your grocery store.)
2-3 tbsp clear vanilla, to taste
2 lbs powdered sugar

Directions
1. Sift the powdered sugar
2. In large mixing bowl, combine everything but the powdered sugar and mix for 1-2 minutes.
3. Gradually add the sugar until the icing is smooth. (The longer you mix it, the smoother it will become.)

Remember never to frost cupcakes that are going into the freezer. Instead, wait until the day of your sale. Some people even haul the cupcakes unfrosted and then once they arrive at the event, quickly frost them. This reduces the chances of messing them up in a bumpy car ride.

Obviously, there are too many variations of sweet baked goods for me to give you a recipe for everything, but I'd like to give you two more recipes for items that sell well. A baked fudge recipe and a cookie recipe that will have people knocking down your doors. (Sorry, my famous brownie recipe isn't up for grabs!)

Baked Fudge

Candy is always a hot seller at events, but in order to comply with most cottage laws, you'll have to sell a fudge that's been baked because it contains milk and is perishable. But don't worry—this recipe from Food.com checks every box and is delicious.

Simple but Decadent Fudge

This recipe comes directly from a chef and produces mouthwatering fudge that is sure to sell. You can make it your own by adding different flavors like peanut butter, white chocolate, or different nuts. The possibilities are endless!

Ingredients:
4 eggs, beaten
2 cups sugar
½ flour
½ cup cocoa
1 cup melted butter
1 cup chopped pecans
1 ¾ tsp vanilla extract
¼ tsp sale

Directions:
1. Beat eggs until they're the color of lemons
2. Add them to the dry ingredients and mix well.
3. Add the butter and stir in the rest of the ingredients.
4. Pour batter into an 8 x 12 inch pan
5. Set that pan into a larger pan that is filled with water.
6. Bake at 325 degrees for 45-50 minutes or until it's set like a custard.

Cookies

Finally, here's a sugar cookie recipe from Allrecipes that you can easily make your own by adding various spices, candies, icing or other toppings. Don't hold back—get creative!

Basic Sugar Cookie Recipe
Yields 48 cookies

Ingredients:
2 ¾ cups all-purpose flour
1 tsp baking soda
½ tsp baking powder
1 cup butter, softened
1 ½ cup sugar
1 egg
1 tsp vanilla extract

Directions:
1. Preheat the oven to 375 degrees F.
2. Using a small bowl, mix together the flour, baking soda, and baking powder. Set it aside.
3. Using a large bowl, cream together the sugar and butter until it's smooth. Then beat in the egg and vanilla extract, and then slowly add in the dry ingredients.
4. Roll the dough into balls and place on cookie sheets.
5. Bake for 8 to 10 minutes or until golden brown.
6. After two minutes, remove from cookie sheet and cool on wire racks.
7. If using icing, wait until completely cool.

Bread

Okay, is your sweet tooth satisfied? I hope so because we're going to move on to another type of baked good that sells wonderfully at all types of events: freshly baked bread. And with this homemade product, the possibilities are literally endless. Here's a list of some of your options:

Bagel	Soda bread
Baguette	Rye bread
Beer bread	Monkey bread
Biscuits	Muffins
Bolillo	Naan
Boule	Olive bread
Challah	Pita
Ciabatta	Pizza
Cornbread	Potato bread
Crackers	Pretzels
Croissant	Pumpernickel bread
Flatbreads	Scones
Focaccia	Sourdough bread
French bread	Tortillas
Gluten free bread	

As you can see, the choice of breads is just about as large as the sweet's list. And I've only listed the most popular and well-known types of breads—you may have a family recipe for a different type of bread that may sell like hotcakes!

You can sell breads at farmer's markets (hugely popular!), online, to local people in your area, or if your cottage laws allow it, to nearby restaurants or specialty shops. Don't forget about the ever popular gluten free breads if your set up allows it. (You have to be very careful not to contaminate with gluten because people with sensitivities can get very sick.)

You'll need to select your bread depending on where you plan to sell it and what kind of pricing it can bring. For instance, although artesian breads are in vogue right now, they are expensive to make. If you sell an olive oil, Kalamata olive bread, your ingredients are going to be expensive no matter where you source them. That's why many bakers stick to the simple bread recipes, like the one I've listed below. But if your market supports it, by all means make artesian breads to supply willing customers. Remember, you can always adjust your offerings, depending on what your experiences are for each type of market you sell to.

Here's an easy to make recipe for a white loaf from allrecipes.

Simple Farmer's Loaf
Yields 1 loaf

Ingredients
2 cups warm water
6 ½ cups flour
1 tsp salt
⅓ cup butter, diced and chilled

Directions
1. Dissolve yeast in warm water in a small bowl. Let it stand for about 10 minutes.
2. Combine 4 cups of the flour and the salt in a large bowl. Cut in the butter and stir in the yeast mixture.
3. Beat in the remaining flour ½ cup at a time. When the dough is mixed, knead it on a lightly floured surface for about 10 minutes. (Until it's smooth and elastic).
4. Butter a large bowl and put the dough in it, turning it to coat it. Cover it with a damp cloth

and let it rise for about an hour. The dough should double in size.

5. Preheat the oven to 400 degrees F. Lightly great a large baking sheet.

6. Deflate the dough and put it on a lightly floured surface. Form it into a large oval loaf and put it in the prepared pan. Cover it again with the cloth for about 30 minutes, or until it has doubled in size again.

7. Once the dough is risen, cut a ½ inch deep cross on the top of it, and then brush it with water.

8. Bake for 25 minutes, and then reduce oven temperature to 350 degrees F. At that temperature, bake for 15 minutes, or until the bottom of the loaf sounds hollow when tapped.

In addition to various types of bread loafs, there are plenty of other things customers love to buy. Soft pretzels always attract a crowd, and luckily, are fairly easy to make. Here's a great recipe from Grandma Bees Recipes.

Soft Pretzels
Yields 12 pieces

Ingredients
2 ½ tsp yeast (or 1 pkg.)
2 tbsp brown sugar
1 ½ cup warm water
1 tsp salt
4 cups unbleached flour

Directions

1. Combine yeast, brown sugar, and warm water in a mixing bowl. Let sit until yeast has dissolved and is bubbly. Add the flour and salt and stir with a wooden spoon until mixed.

2. Put the dough onto a lightly floured surface and knead for 5 minutes or until smooth and elastic. Put the dough into a greased bowl and cover it with a cloth. Let rise for 45 minutes. It's ready when you stick your finger in the middle of the dough and your fingerprint remains.

3. Divide the dough into 12 equal pieces and roll them into a thin, long rope about 24 inches long. Twist each piece into a pretzel shape.

4. Spray a baking sheet with non-stick spray, then line with parchment paper. Place pretzels on sheet and let sit for 10 minutes.

5. While dough is resting, bring 4 cups water and $\frac{1}{4}$ cup of baking soda to a boil in a shallow pan.

6. Put one of the dough pretzels into the mixture and wait 15 seconds, while spooning the mixture over it.

7. Using a spatula, remove the pretzel from the soda bath and place on a paper towel to absorb the liquid.

8. After all pretzels have been bathed in the liquid, return them to the baking sheet and brush each an egg wash (1 egg yolk, beaten and 1 tsp of water). Then sprinkle them with course sale.

9. Preheat oven to 450 degrees F. Allow pretzels to rest while the oven is heating.

10. Bake pretzels for 8 minutes or until golden brown.

Jams, Jellies, and Salsas

In addition to pastries and breads, homemade canned goods always attract a lot of attention from shoppers. You're only limited by your imagination if you want to sell canned goods because with the tweak of a recipe or the addition of one spice, you can change the game.

But when you sell homemade canned goods, you'll have to be very careful because if you do it wrong, you could make someone sick. That's why I recommend that you only use recipes given by the experts. My favorite is Ball, which publishes a fantastic cookbook. In fact, in May of this year, they released their newest edition called *The All New Ball Book of Canning and Preserving: Over 350 of the Best Canned, Jammed, Pickled, and Preserved Recipes.*

Unlike the other product ideas in this book, I'm not going to give you adapted recipes—it's just not safe. Instead, I've scoured the Ball recipe selections and have provided you with three of the most interesting ones I found. I'm giving them to you *exactly* as they're printed in order to avoid any mistakes. I highly recommend that if you want to sell canned or preserved goods, you buy the cookbook and choose from one of the hundreds of great recipes in it.

But for now, how about starting with a popular favorite—homemade dill pickles.

Kosher Dill Pickles

Preserving Method: Water bath Canning, Fresh Preserve method, which stores for up to 1 year.
Makes about 2 Quarts

Ingredients:

3 ½ lbs pickling cucumbers (about 14 small to medium)
2 cups water
1 cup vinegar (5% acidity)
¼ cup Ball® Kosher Dill Pickle Mix
2 Ball® Quart (32 oz) Fresh Preserving Jars with lids and bands

Directions

1. Cut ends off cucumbers. Cut into spears.
2. Combine water, vinegar, and Ball® Kosher Dill Pickle Mix in a medium saucepan. Heat to a boil.
3. Prepare canner, jars, and lids according to manufacturer's instructions.
4. Pack spears into hot jars. Ladle hot pickling liquid over spears leaving ½ inch headspace. Remove air bubbles. Wipe rims. Center lids on jars. Apply bands and adjust to fingertip tight. Place jar in boiling water canner. Repeat until all jars are filled.
5. Process jars for 15 minutes, adjusting for altitude. Turn off heat; remove lid and let jars stand 5 minutes. Remove jars and cool. Check for seal after 24 hours. Lids should not flex up and down when center is pressed.

QUICK TIP: For best flavor, allow pickles to stand 4-6 weeks.

If you'd rather sell sweet canned goods, how about this peach ginger butter. Would *you* pass it up at a farmer's market?

Peach Ginger Butter

Preserving method: water bath canning
Makes 6 half-pint jars

Ingredients
10 cups coarsely chopped fresh peaches (about 12 medium)
1/2 cup water
1/2 cup finely chopped crystallized ginger
2 tsp. lemon zest
2 Tbsp. fresh lemon juice
3 cups sugar

Directions
1. Combine first 5 ingredients in a 6-qt. stainless steel or enameled Dutch oven. Bring to a boil over medium-high heat, stirring often. Reduce heat, and simmer, uncovered, 15 minutes or until peaches are tender, stirring occasionally. Remove from heat, and let cool slightly.
2. Pulse peach mixture, in batches, in a food processor until almost smooth. Pour each batch into a large bowl.
3. Return peach puree to Dutch oven; stir in sugar. Bring to a boil over medium heat, stirring until sugar dissolves. Cook, stirring constantly, 25 to 30 minutes or until mixture thickens and holds its shape on a spoon.
4. Ladle hot peach mixture into a hot jar, leaving 1/4-inch headspace. Remove air bubbles. Wipe jar rim. Center lid on jar. Apply band, and adjust to fingertip-tight. Place jar in boiling-water canner.

Repeat until all jars are filled.
5. Process jars 10 minutes, adjusting for altitude.
Turn off heat; remove lid, and let jars stand 5
minutes. Remove jars and cool.

And for those of you who love a good salsa, you
can't go wrong with this one. You can use any kind of
chili peppers you prefer in it so you can make it your
own signature salsa.

Zesty Salsa

Preserving method: water bath canning
Makes about 6 (16 oz) pints or 12 (8 oz) half pint

Ingredients
10 cups chopped cored peeled tomatoes
(about 25 medium)
5 cups chopped seeded green bell peppers
(about 4 large)
5 cups chopped onions (about 6 to 8 medium)
2-½ cups chopped seeded chili peppers, such as
hot banana, Hungarian wax, serrano or jalapeño
(about 13 medium)
1-¼ cups cider vinegar
3 cloves garlic, finely chopped
2 Tbsp finely chopped cilantro
1 Tbsp salt
1 tsp hot pepper sauce, optional
6 16 oz pint or 12 8 oz half pint glass preserving
jars with lids and bands.

Directions

1. Prepare boiling water canner. Heat jars in simmering water until ready for use. Do not boil. Wash lids in warm soapy water and set bands aside.

2. Combine tomatoes, green peppers, onions, chili peppers, vinegar, garlic, cilantro, salt and hot pepper sauce, if using, in a large stainless steel saucepan. Bring to a boil over medium-high heat, stirring constantly. Reduce heat and boil gently, stirring frequently, until slightly thickened, about 10 minutes.

3. Ladle hot salsa into hot jars, leaving ½ inch headspace. Remove air bubbles and adjust headspace, if necessary, by adding hot salsa. Wipe rim. Center lid on jar. Apply band until fit is fingertip tight.

4. Process both pint and half pint jars in a boiling water canner for 15 minutes, adjusting for altitude. Remove jars and cool. Check lids for seal after 24 hours. Lid should not flex up and down when center is pressed.

Don't forget, you can do jams and jellies of all types, different salsas, barbecue sauces, preserves, fruit butters, roasted vegetables, compotes, and more. Just make sure that you use a proven recipe by someone in the business who has tested it thoroughly.

In addition to the products listed above, there are other types of foods you can easily provide to hungry customers. Home-based vendors across the country are selling seasoned nuts and popcorn, along with other items such as freshly roasted coffee and candied apples.

All of these products have a place in the market, and if you can carve out your own niche with them, you'll likely find that you don't have much competition.

Just for fun, here's a recipe for candied pecans, but you could use it for any nuts. Unlike some other complicated recipes, this one is quick and simple— something you'll come to appreciate when you're making up dozens of bags for an event the next morning. The recipe comes from Twohealthykitchens.

Candied Pecans

These delicious pecans are simple to make and don't require a lot of expensive ingredients (except the pecans)

Ingredients
1½ tablespoons packed brown sugar
1½ teaspoons water
⅛ tsp vanilla
⅛ tsp kosher salt
1 cup pecan halves

Directions
1. Combine brown sugar, water, vanilla, and kosher salt in a small bowl. Stir it to combine, but the sugar and salt won't all dissolve. Set the bowl next to the stove.
2. In a medium-large saucepan over medium heat, toast the pecans for 2-3 minutes or until you smell a nutty aroma. Stir them occasionally so they won't burn.
3. Quickly drizzle the sugar mixture into the pan,

and stir the nuts as you drizzle. Don't stop stirring until the pecans are thoroughly coated in the sugar mixture. Remove the pan from heat so the nuts don't burn.

Spread the pecans on a piece of parchment to cool. Once they're cooled, you can break them apart, if you need to.

Store nuts in an airtight container. They will be slightly sticky at first, but the sugar coating will harden within a few hours.

Did all of this give you a few ideas about what you should sell? Even if you think you know exactly which product you want to produce, you should do a little more research by going to the place where you want to sell and see what others are doing. For example, if you want to sell roasted coffee beans at your local farmer's market, attend it a few times to make sure no one else is already doing it. And if you want to sell cakes or cupcakes to the neighborhood moms, ask around and make sure that need isn't already being met by someone else.

Once you've definitely decided on your product, it's time to get busy creating your brand. This is perhaps one of the most important aspects of designing your business because it will make the first impression on your potential customers.

Are you ready? Let's design your brand—and your future.

Food Business Secret Ingredient No. 2: Use the Tools of the Trade

When running a food business, you'll need to make the best use of your time. Many new business owners don't take their time into account when planning, but the goal of any business owner should be to work the least amount of time possible for the maximum rewards. When working in the food business, there are some great tools that can help you save time while baking. For instance, you'll often need to double recipes, and instead of figuring it out on your own, you can use the simple chart from ThisFoodThing.com. Also, Joy of Baking provides a free pan conversion chart when you aren't sure what size pan to use for the amount of product you're baking. Finally, if you're a cake baker, BakingiT.com is a free tool that is simply awesome. It provides you with calculators that help you design your cake from start to finish.

CHAPTER FOUR:

How to Design a Food Brand That Sells

In today's world, food isn't just food. Instead, most people think of food as an experience. They want more than good taste—they want a story, an interactive experience, a *reason* to eat it.

Don't believe me? Let's take a look at a restaurant that has turned the order of things upside down. Chipotle took a lot of heat when they first opened because they did things differently than most other chains. The chain concentrated on healthy eating, and eventually reconfigured its menu to include non- GMO items. Millennials flocked to the restaurant, in part because of its bold stance on how food should be served, but also because of the quirky things promoted there, like the haiku contests where diners have a chance to win prizes for the best haiku written to a burrito.

Another great example is Chick-fil-A. This restaurant is run by Christians and despite the fact that all their competitors are open on Sundays, they've made it a point to close down that day so their employees can take the day to worship. In addition, the founders of the fast food chain openly talk about their beliefs. If you don't think they've developed a following because of it, just think back to a few years ago when social media drove thousands of customers to Chick-fil-A's across the country on a single day in order to support them in a fight against some Obamacare rules that contradicted their faith.

But these rules don't just apply to national chains and restaurants. In order to create a truly successful home-based business, you'll need to set yourself apart from the local competition so customers will not only remember your food, but also that special "something" about your business. How do you do this? By branding and positioning your business.

What is Food Business Branding?

In the abstract, a brand consists of everything you do, say, and (publically) believe as you represent your business. For instance, do you advertise that you only use organic ingredients, or do you unabashedly admit that your product contains all the bad for you, but oh so good ingredients that make it taste so good? Do you offer a portion of sales to charity, or do you use fun, quirky sayings on your labels? All of these types of actions contribute to a business' brand.

The results of branding are what make you think "homey" when you think of Betty Crocker, "environmentally aware" when you think about Organic Valley, and "comfort" when you think of Kraft. The images that you conjure up when thinking about these brands don't just happen by accident, they're a direct result of the company's efforts to cause you to associate the feelings and emotions with their products. In essence, branding is how a company carves out a niche for their product.

This is true for food businesses, and any other business that markets to consumers. But unlike national corporations, you won't have the same resources and outlets available to get your message to the masses. (Unless you decide to go big—more about that later.) So how do home-based producers brand their products?

One tiny step at a time.

Rather than just give you a list of the things you'll need to do to brand your business, let's take a look at them one by one.

Step 1: Do Market Research

Before you can determine exactly which type of food business you want to start, you'll need to check out the competition in the area to ensure you don't try to start a business in a niche that's already saturated. For example, cupcakes have been hot for the past few years, and if that's your passion, you'll need to make sure there's room in your area for one more cupcake business. The same holds true to any type of food business. Are the wedding planners overrun with solicitations from specialty cake businesses or it that a niche you can fill? Do the local specialty stores already have shelves lined with homemade preserves? Then you'd better look elsewhere. Are the local barbeque restaurants willing to take on a homemade line of sauce? If so, then that's your ticket.

After you've identified the local competition, it's time to check them out. If they sell a product similar to what you want to sell at a local market, buy some and taste it from a customer's standpoint. Could it be improved or would it be difficult to beat? Are they friendly or easy to book an appointment with, or do they refuse to return phone calls?

Take all this information in because you'll need it as you build your business.

Step 2: Decide on Your Niche

Studies have shown that when consumers are faced with a lot of choices, it sometimes makes them leave without making a purchase. That's the last thing you want for your business. So, rather than offering a dizzying array of products, tastes, and choices to your customers, it makes more sense to focus on what you do best. You can always add to your product line as you continue to grow and get to know your customers.

For example, if you make the world's best mini lemon pound cakes and you want to sell them at the farmer's market, why not introduce yourself to the world as that? You can fill the lemon pound cake niche, and then as you develop a following, add a few more flavors, one at a time. The alternative would be to take a smorgasbord of baked goods to the market your first time and get lost in a sea of average, unoriginal bakers.

Why not stop reading right now and jot down what your specialty is? Do you have a recipe people can't stop talking about? If so, start there and build. Have you always wanted to take your cake decorating skills to market? Then that's your niche.

But what if you don't have that special recipe or any idea of what niche you want to carve out for yourself? Then it's time to start dreaming. Go ahead, put down this book and begin to dream about what niche you want to excel in. Don't limit yourself by what you can do right now because you can always learn. Do you want to sell artesian breads, but don't know how to bake them? Don't let that stop you. Write it down and work towards the goal of learning to make the best artesian breads you can. Remember, if someone else can bake a wonderful olive and red pepper artesian bread, so can you. It may take a lot of practice and trial and error, but you'll get it.

And remember, it's important to check chapter ten to determine which types of foods your state allows home cooks to sell.

Step 3: Identify Your Ideal Customer

You next step in the process is perhaps one of the most important: you must identify who your target market is, or to put it simply, your ideal customer. Many newbies in the food business believe that their product appeals to everyone and so their target market is "everyone." But that's a huge mistake in a food business (or any business for that matter) and if you go in with that attitude, it will seriously affect your ability to market and promote your business.

Here are the benefits to pinpointing who your ideal/target customer is:

- It will help you get the best ROI (return on investment) for your advertising efforts because if you understand who you're appealing to, you'll better know how to reach them.

- It will help you create your name and your slogan.

- It will help you choose where to sell your product.

- It will determine the price you set for your product.

Pretty important stuff, huh? But how do you know who your ideal customer is if you've never sold a product? The mega companies use data and experts and spend thousands of dollars to identify their target markets, but I'm guessing you don't have those kinds of resources.

Relax, there are other ways to approach this. To start, you'll need to make a list of what benefits people will get by using your products. Let's imagine that you sell organic artesian breads. People who purchase your product will get the following benefits:

- The ability to eat or serve their family organic bread that doesn't contain the harmful chemicals that commercial breads do.

- The good feeling that comes from supporting the local food community.

- Eating bread that is freshly baked, which tastes much better than store bought bread.

- The convenience of buying fresh bread instead of having to make it themselves.

That's a lot of benefits for the people who would buy your bread. Now, the next step is to determine which types of people *want* those benefits.

- Busy moms who want to feed their families organic, healthy food.

- People who support the buy local movement.

- People who love the taste of good, artesian bread.

- People who like fresh bread, but don't have time or knowledge to make it themselves.

Adding all of this up, your target market would be moms who appreciate good bread and organic foods and want to feed it to their families, but don't have the time or knowledge to make it themselves. They also love to buy from local vendors.

Now, I'm not saying that dads or others won't appreciate and buy artesian breads, but judging from the two lists above, it seems that those moms who fall under this category would likely be the bulk of the business. Of course, other types of people would likely buy the breads too, but they wouldn't make up the bulk of sales. That's why most advertising would need to be directed to the moms who fit the profile.

Once you've completed this exercise, you'll have a good idea of who your ideal customer is without having to spend the thousands of dollars that the mega food corporations do.

It's time to sit down and think about your own food product. First, make a list of all the benefits people can get from purchasing it, and then make another list of who would likely seek out those benefits. Put them all together and write out a description of your ideal customer.

Now, don't you feel more prepared to take the next step?

Step 4: Name Your Business

What's in a name? Absolutely everything. Your business name is the first impression potential customers will have of your business. It's your offered handshake to the world, your "hello" to every passerby, and the first thing that may get them to stop and take a second look.

Knowing that, getting your name right is absolutely critical.

Business owners generally take two roads when it comes to naming their business. Some use the opportunity to catch the attention of their potential customers by making the name stand out, tell a story, or make them think. Others choose a generic name that could be found in any city in the world. In other words, if it's safe, your customers are likely to forget it within minutes. Which do you think would help you build a profitable food business?

A good business name should have all of the following components:

- It should grab people's attention and make them want to know more about your products.

- It should convey your brand promise. Is your promise the crunchiest dill pickles they've ever had? (think Crunch Time Homemade Pickles) Or will you sell the most decadent truffle salt they can image? (Pure Extravagance Truffle Salt) Whatever your brand's promise is, put it in your name!

- Align it with your core customer's mind set. Make sure you're speaking to your ideal customers with your business name. For example, if you're selling the high end truffle salt referenced above, the words "Pure Extravagance" will speak to your buyers.

- In short, your business name should sum up your brand in a way that everyone who sees it will instantly understand what your food business is all about.

Let me give you some more examples. Let's imagine that your name is Susie and you sell cupcakes. If you're like a lot of cupcake business owners, you'll simply use your personal name and call the business Susie's Cupcakes. That's cute, but what does it tell potential customers about your business? All they'll learn from that name is that your name is Susie and you sell cupcakes.

But what if you took your specialty and made a business brand name with it? Imagine that Susie specialized in savory cupcakes. She could call her business Susie's Savory Cupcakes and customers would instantly understood what she had to offer. Or imagine that she sold cupcakes that were loaded with buttercream frosting. Why not call it Top Heavy Buttercream Cupcakes & More?

Get the picture? If you've already decided which niche you'll fill and who your target customer is, it's time to get to work on your name. It may come to you instantly, or it may take weeks to nail it down, but however long it takes, don't settle until you're sure you've found just the right one.

Now, let's move on the next important aspect of branding your business.

Step 5: Tell Your Food Story

Remember how we talked about you needing that something "special" to differentiate yourself from your competitors? One of the best ways to get across that message is with your food story.

What is a food story? It's what will make customers understand why your product is better than what they can find in the grocery aisles. It's the story of why your prices are a little higher, why they should trust in you as the baker or processor, where the raw products came from, why it's healthier or better tasting that other people's, and so on. In other words, it's the story the customer will take back home with them and tell at the dinner table while people are enjoying your delicious food.

Let me give you an example.

As I told you earlier, I bake. Now I don't exactly look like a baker, and many people may be hesitant to try my brownies because of it. But my story usually causes them to get past those fears and buy my products anyway. What's my story?

Well, for starters, I immediately deal with the elephant in the room—that's me—and use signage and wear a tee-shirt that proclaims "Real Men Bake Brownies." (That's true, by the way.)

It's an instant ice-breaker and does a couple of things. For starters, it makes people notice me and take note of my company. And most of the time, even if they weren't thinking about eating a brownie at that moment, they come to my table because they want to hear more.

And that's when they hear my story.

You see, I'm just an average guy who has the ability to bake some pretty fantastic brownies. But that's not all. I'm a fanatic about using organic, locally sourced ingredients and will proudly tell anyone who asks which local dairy farm I use, cite my organic cocoa source, or that I use the eggs from my own organically raised chickens in the recipe.

Now, can you image someone taking home my brownies and telling their family or dinner guests about the "Real Man" who baked them? That's my story—what's yours?

Here are the key elements you'll need to include in your story:

- Why should customers go out of their way to come and purchase products from you? (Do you use organic or gluten free ingredients, do you donate a portion of the profits to a local charity, is everything sourced locally, or has the recipe been handed down for three generations in your family?) Remember, most customers who buy from you want to know where their food comes from and feel connected to the source of that food.

- Your story must explain why your food is better or different than what they can find at their local grocer. Do you make potato chips without the chemicals? Tell them about it in your story.

- Your story should also make them feel a part of the experience. For instance, if you source your fruit from a local orchard, provide photos of it, or provide them with brochures showing the grounds and a number to call for a private tour. If you partner with a nonprofit, explain to customers what impact their purchase will make.

- Your story should begin a conversation with your customers. If you sell canned goods made from the vegetables and fruits grown in your garden, talk to them about your refusal to use pesticides and even provide them a photo to two of your garden.

In short, your story should make the customer feel as if they're getting a product that is fresh, traceable, authentic, and produced with integrity. And don't forget, if you use a sign, tee-shirt, or other method to spark consumer's curiosity, like my Real Men Bake Brownies signs and tee-shirts, you'll oftentimes have a chance to tell your story where you might not have otherwise.

Step 6: Use Packaging to Brand Your Product

When it comes to packaging your product, you'll have a ton of options. You can go sophisticated, cutesy, fun, earthy, or any other theme you want to use. And you won't have a shortage of packaging supplies to choose from either. (I provide you a generous list in a future chapter of this book.)

But the one thing you shouldn't forget is that your packaging should tell the story of your brand. What do I mean?

Let's imagine that you sell organic savory cupcakes made only of the purest and finest ingredients. In order to stay with your brand, you should choose an earthy themed package to put them in. Maybe a natural looking brown or green wrapped in twine, or something along those lines. What you shouldn't do is package your natural product in a brightly colored package or one made of plastic or other synthetic materials.

On the other hand, if your brand is fun and quirky, your packaging should reflect that. In this circumstance, brightly colored packaging would fit the bill, as would funky names for each product and tags with clever sayings tied to the package.

If you have a high-end product, your packaging should reflect that, too. For instance, our truffle salt should be packaged in a way that makes customers feel as if they're getting their money's worth for the high-end product. But if you're selling inexpensive cupcakes at a farmer's market, you can easily get away with short plastic cups wrapped in clear gift bags and tied with a ribbon.

Just remember your brand should remain consistent for the customer with every interaction they have with you and your product, and your packaging plays a major role in that vision.

Step 7: Use a Logo to Further Identify Your Brand

Another part of your packaging that will help get your story across to customers is the logo you design for your business, along with the tagline you use. Let's take a look at each and talk about how to choose the right one, and what to do with them.

Most businesses have a logo, a readily identifiable symbol that makes it easy for consumers to recognize a product. Perhaps one of the best know is the Morton Salt girl. She is standing in rain to symbolize that the salt won't clump, not even in the rain. The Laughing Cow cheese is another logo that most people recognize with its red cow laughing and wearing a pair of earrings made out of the cheese. Both of these logos have remained the same since their inception, but for a few modifications to update them throughout the years. And each logo portrays what the business is about.

The Morton Salt logo was designed to let customers know they could feel safe using their product even on wet, sticky days because it wouldn't clump. And The Laughing Cow logo was designed when the owner of the new company, who was a French cheesemaker, hired a soon to be famous cartoon artist to create a logo that put a spin on Norse mythology because he wanted a lighthearted logo and name for his cheese.

So, what about your food brand? How can you best express it so customers will instantly know what you're all about? You can either create the logo yourself at places like makelogoonlinefree.com, where you can design a logo by editing one of thousands of designs, GraphicSprings.com, where you can create a logo and download the file for under $20 if you decide you like it, or LogoGarden.com, where you can create a logo and download it for free.

If you don't have the skills to create your own logo, you can also outsource the job fairly inexpensively. TheLogoCompany.net is a full-service logo company that will design your logo for $199. And if you prefer to work directly with a freelancer, UpWork.com is the best place to find them.

Just for some inspiration before you begin designing your logo, here are five things you should know:

- Choose your colors wisely. Color is the backbone of any brand, and your logo should reflect the colors you've chosen for your brand. But when designing a logo, it's important that it looks just as good in grayscale as it does in color for those marketing instances when black and white is your only option.

- Make it unique. If you take a look at some food industry logos, you'll quickly realize that many of them are just generic versions of the same design. Be bold with your design and make it uniquely your own. If you keep your story in mind while designing it (or tell a designer about it), it can't help but be unique.

- Don't use a standard font. You don't want to use a font that every other business uses for its logo. Instead, think outside the box and pick a font that you don't often see. It will need to be easily read, and fit in with your story. Other than that, get creative with it!

- Don't try and do too much. Simplicity is the rule for well thought out logos, and yours should make a bold statement with simplicity. If you need a visual, just think of Justin's nut butters and the jars with a symbol of a nut on them. Or conjure up images of Apple's logo— an apple with a bit taken out of it. Simple, but brilliant.

- Consider using motion. When a logo has an implied motion, such as Twitter's flying bird, it implies forward moving. Yours might be a bakery truck on the move, a whisk that looks like it's in action, or a cupcake with a bite taken out and crumbs falling. The idea is to create a unique logo that will catch people's attention.

Step 8: Use the Right Tagline to Help Brand Your Business

Now that you have some guidance about your logo, let's talk about your tagline. A tagline is your company's message or mission statement summed up in just a few words. Some examples are Mary's Gone Crackers' tagline of "Conscious Eating," or Numi's Organic Tea's tagline of "Celebrating People, Planet, and Pure Tea." Both of these lines tell consumers what the company is about and what they can expect when purchasing the product.

What about yours? Do you preserve fruit butters using only homegrown produce? Your tagline could read, "Homegrown means better butters." Or do you sell candied pecans and donate portions of your profits to an orphanage? Your tagline could be "We're nuts about kids and your purchase helps support them."

Creating a tagline is serious business because just any old sentence won't do. It takes a good sense of what your business offers, a solid idea of what you want your business to represent to the world, and a firm grasp of what makes your food company different.

Still not convinced you need a tagline? Here are four reasons why you should create a well-thought out tagline as part of your branding:

- It will attract the attention of browsers and even people who may not be specifically looking to buy in that instant.

- It helps create a cohesive brand for your food business.

- It makes it easier for people to memorize your company name.

- It allows you to make a bold statement about your business' mission and values.

When writing your tagline, there some specific things to keep in mind so you'll create a statement that will make consumers take notice. Here are four of the most important ones.

- **Use it to differentiate yourself from your competitors.** To do that, identify the main thing that makes your product better than other similar products, and highlight it. For example, in our fruit butters example above, the fact that the fruits are homegrown is highlighted in the tagline.

- **Use it to show your commitment to customers.** In all likelihood, you'll be selling the same products other home producers do, even if you put your own twist on them. One great use of a tagline is to show customers what your commitment is to them. For example, if you sell custom cakes, your tagline could be "We're passionate about baking the perfect cake for you."

- **Be brief.** The best taglines are 8 words or less and are never longer than 1 sentence. Keep drilling down your idea until it's in the shortest sentence possible.

- **Make it rhythm**. Studies have shown that taglines that rhythm are more memorable to consumers. You could have fun with this one while showcasing your commitment and uniqueness. For instance, We Bake the Best Cake (in town).

Of course, not everyone is going to be able to write their own tagline and that's okay because there are online tools that will help you generate, if not the perfect line, one close enough that you can improve it. For example, the Shopify Free Slogan Maker gives you plenty of options to choose from after you type in a keyword, Sloganizer.net gives you one free slogan every time you type in a keyword, and Procato.com also offers a slogan generator tool that's easy to use.

Step 9: Showcase Your Brand with the Right Display

Packaging isn't the only thing you'll need to pay attention to in the marketing of your brand. The way your display your product will also have a huge impact on how successful your business is because customers will use your displays to determine whether or not to buy from you.

For example, if you're selling baked goods at a farmer's market, you'll have a table like everyone else, but how will you use that table to display your goods? That depends on your brand. If you're branding is home style goodness, you might use wooden crates and mini wooden ladders to display your goods on. On the other hand, if your branding is more like a French bakery, you could use pink shelving and bakery cases with black lettering.

The same holds true no matter what type of product you produce. A nuts vendor could use brown paper bags with a simple logo on it, tied together with twine for a natural brand, or a clear cone bags with gold ties and a spectacular label for fancy nuts.

If you're a cake baker who specializes in weddings, then display your cakes in pretty glass cake stands and have photos in frames on the table showing off some of your more successful wedding cakes. If you do cupcakes for children's parties, set up a "decorate your own cupcake" booth for kids, and then hand out brochures to their parents.

As you can see, your display is only limited by your imagination, but it's important because it's the final detail in a well thought out brand.

Keep it Consistent

Now that you have a solid idea of how you want to brand your business, I need you to make me a promise, okay? Never, ever deviate from your brand when you're creating, packaging, displaying or talking about your product. Your brand is everything when it comes to your success, and I can't stress this enough.

Let me give you an example. Let's say one day in my brownie business I find some baby blue packaging on sale so I decide to save a few bucks. Instead of using my manly black brownie boxes with my cool logo, I put the brownies in the blue boxes and go to my regular market to sell. Two things will happen. First, my regular customers will be confused because in a week, I'd gone from just about the coolest brownie seller around to one who has no brand. After all, without the familiar packaging and logo, who am I besides just another shmuck peddling brownies?

Secondly, new customers just aren't going to "get" me. The "story" would be gone and they would no longer have a compelling reason to buy from me.

The same will happen to you and your business if you deviate from your brand, especially once it's established.

So don't do it, okay? Trust me, you'll thank me later when your food business is booming.

Food Business Secret Ingredient No. 3: Defining Your Secret Sauce

Don't forget when branding your food business that you need one special something that will differentiate your products from everyone else's. Ideally, you'll identify that "something" before you choose your name, design your labels, or choose your packaging. Your secret sauce may be in your ingredients, the story of your company, or what you do with your profits, but you need something to make customers remember you.

CHAPTER FIVE:

The Well Stocked Food Business: What You Need to Become a Success

Are you getting excited? Can't you just feel it—that "something" in the air that promises you're about to embark on an adventure that will lead to an entirely new lifestyle?

That's the fresh scent of success, and it's permeating the air just like that fresh pot of coffee you brew every morning. Breathe in deeply. Can't you just smell it?

But in order to succeed in a food business, you need the right tools. In this chapter, we'll talk about what you need to start and grow your business into the company you dream about.

But before we start, we need to discuss the mundane: the licenses and permits your state requires you to have before you open your business. If you haven't already checked chapter ten where I list each state's requirements, please do so now. Some states will require that you take a simple online food handling course, and then you'll be free to open your doors. Others will require kitchen inspections, zoning clearances, and permits before you can begin selling. Simply look up your state in the back of this book, and you'll find all the information you need.

And now for the fun part—taking about the equipment you'll need to get up and running in your home-based food business.

The Tools of the Trade

Let's start in the kitchen. Since you'll be making all of your goodies there, you've got to make sure it's equipped with all you need. Now, I realize that not everyone will be producing the same type of food, so the required equipment is going to vary. But here are some things that every food business requires.

- Space. You're going to be making a lot of food, and you'll need enough space to support the process. For example, if you're making cupcakes or other baked goods, you'll need enough counter space to prepare the dough, an oven, and an area set aside for cooling racks once the cakes come out of the oven. You'll also need an area to frost and decorate your creations.

- Storage. What are you going to do with 100 homemade jars of jam? What about 20 meticulously decorated cakes? You'll need to have a storage space, whether it be your freezer for cupcakes made the day before market, or a shelving area to hold 200 bags of kettle corn. And in addition to storing your finished product, you'll also need to store your raw ingredients. For example, do you have room to store 50 pound bags of flour and sugar?

- Equipment. Every type of home cook needs some sort of equipment to produce their food, and what you'll need depends on what you plan to make. For example, if you're going to sell baked goods, you'll might need a good mixer, cookie cutters, piping bags and tips, rolling pins, pans and tins, measuring cups and spoons, sifters, cooling racks, candy molds, and packaging. If you're a canner, you'll need either a water bath or pressure canner, jars, lids, and cooking racks. Nut sellers will need lots of baking sheets and maybe even a double oven.

Transportation

So, have you thought about how you'll get those 1,000 cupcakes to the farmer's market? Or that wedding cake that took you all day to decorate to the wedding? You'll need a car, truck, or van that is big enough to carry your goods to the marketplace. Whether you plan to use your own car or buy one, you might consider having the business purchase the car so you can use it as a write off to help lower your tax bill.

In addition to the automobile, you'll need carrying cases to pack your product in so it's not destroyed during the ride. Can you imagine spending hours decorating 500 cupcakes, only to have them fall into each other on the ride, ruining all your hard work?

Some of the transporting options are obvious. If you are transporting a cake, carefully put in a cake box and make sure it's supported on all sides so it can't slide while you're driving. And if you're transporting bags of popcorn or nuts, simply put them in boxes. Canned goods are also easy because you can use boxes with dividers to transport them easily and without risk of breakage.

But how in the world do you transport hundreds of cupcakes? There are a couple of ways to do this. First, you could pack individual cupcake boxes with inserts and carefully place each one in a larger Tupperware type container. This method will safely get your cupcakes to the end location, but can get expensive when you have to continually purchase boxes and inserts just for transport.

An option is to make your own cupcake "case" by pressing tin foil up against the back of a cupcake muffin pan. Make sure the foil you use is larger than the pan because you'll need to squish it up against the extruding circles. Once you've molded the foil, take it off the back of the pan and use it to "hold" your cupcakes in place. Then put them in the Tupperware type containers and carry them to your destination.

Website

Even if your state doesn't allow you to sell your home cooked goods online, you should still create a website for a couple of reasons. For starters, cottage food laws are changing all the time, and just because you can't sell online today, that doesn't mean the laws won't change. Currently, I'm unable to sell my brownies online, but the legislature meets again in 2017, and I'm hoping it will change so I've prepared myself for the possibility by reserving my domain name.

Secondly, you'll need some sort of online presence to keep customers updated about your comings and goings. For instance, if you're known for your fruit butters and you happen on a large amount of peaches, how will you let your customers know that you're taking peach and vanilla jam to the market this weekend? You can—and should—use social media accounts like Facebook, Twitter, and Instagram to stay current with customers, but it's also important to have a professional looking website for your business.

But it doesn't have to cost a lot of money. For example, my website RainMakerPress.com is where people sign up to receive news about upcoming books in the Work from Home series. The site is very unique and after seeing it, a lot of people sign up. And here's the thing—it cost me nothing to create and $7 a month to keep it up and running.

Having a professional website will set you apart from your competitors and allow consumers to take a look at photos of your gorgeous products online. This is especially important if you plan to sell to private parties such as weddings or birthday parties.

Here's a brief primer on how to set up your website for little to no money.

Select and Purchase Your Domain Name

Your first step in the process is choosing your internet address. Your domain name is the way people will find your website. Ideally, your domain name should be the same as your business name, but that's not always possible. If your business is Gooey Creations, you could try for GooeyCreations.com. If the domain hasn't already been taken, grab it, even if you're not quite ready to set up your website.

If it's already taken, you'll probably be offered a domain with a different extension, such as .net, .biz, or even .food. This can be tricky because most people are conditioned to use the .com extension. I recommend that if possible, you stick with that one, even if you have to adjust your desired domain name. For example, when I went to register SamKerns.com, I was disappointed to find that someone had already claimed it, and so I had to use my publishing name, RainMakerPress.com. I could have registered a name like SamKerns1.com, but really, who's going to remember that?

When deciding on your name, keep these things in mind:

- Don't use a hyphen. It just looks confusing and may cause people to be unable to find your site.

- Keep your name short. Don't fall into the old school trap of using a long name like TheBestCupcakesInTheWholeWideWorld.com. Can you image typing that in every time you wanted to purchase cupcakes?

- Skip the SEO. Search engine optimization is great for getting the content and articles on your website noticed by the search engines, but it doesn't work for domain names anymore. People use to use keywords (or often search for words) as domain names and when someone searched for the word, that website would show up in the first page of the search results. For instance, if your site was named Cupcakes.com and someone typed cupcakes into the search engine, they would see your site. Unfortunately,

Google changed its algorithm and that tactic doesn't work anymore.

You can look to see if your desired domain name is available at GoDaddy or 1and1.com. Both will tell you if your name is available, and if it is, they'll register it for you for .99 cents.

Determine Where to Park Your Domain Name

Okay, now that you have the perfect domain name picked out, you need to find a place to park it. To do that, you'll need to select a web hosting company. Here, you have a couple of options—you can hire a website designer and pay them a lot of money to park and design your site, or you can do it yourself.

Look, I know it's intimidating, but really, it doesn't have to be. Let me walk you through the basics. You can easily whip out an intricate fondant design, can't you? Then this will be a breeze.

Start out by exploring your ecommerce platform options. These handy sites allow you to point, click and drag elements into a website so you can design your own without any prior experience. They will also allow you collect payments and shipping information online if you're lucky enough to live in a state that allows you to sell your goods online.

Here's a list of the platforms you should explore for your site:

- Wix. For only $16.58 a month, you can build a customized ecommerce site with a payment gateway and shopping cart with this host.

- Weebly. If you can't sell your goods online, but want a site that allows you to have a professional presence, you can set up a fully customized site for free on this site. If you can sell online, you'll only pay $25 per month for an ecommerce package that includes a shopping cart. Shopping carts allow your customers to pay you with credit cards or via PayPal.

- Shopify. This platform is easy to use and the prices are hard to beat. They start at $9 per month for one buy button (if you only have one product), and $29 per month for a full online store.

- BigCommerce. For only $29 a month, you can set up your site with this platform. It offers an all-inclusive website with all the tools you need.

- Squarespace. If you're looking for platform that doesn't require a long term commitment, this may be it. Rates start at $26 a month (with no contracts) and you'll get an integrated shopping cart and other important essentials.

- WordPress via BlueHost. If you're on a very tight budget and happen to have some computer skills, you can set up a WordPress site using BlueHost. The platform will host your WordPress site for as little as $3.49 per month. Then you can use WooCommerce to install a free shopping cart.

When designing your website be sure to keep your customers in mind and keep it as simple as possible. Focus on what you want the site to accomplish it and then design it around that. Do you want a site that customers can check to see what flavors you're taking to the next market? Then concentrate on that. Or do you want an online booking system for your cake decorating business? If so, keep that as the focus.

Payment Systems

No matter where you sell your goods, you need a way to accept electronic payments from customers. Sure, some will pay you in cash, especially if you sell $3 cupcakes at a farmer's market, but these days, not everyone carries cash, and most people don't think twice about using their debit card for a $3 purchase. In fact, a recent study shows that 65 percent of people believe that by 2020, mobile payments will replace cash and even credit cards. Other experts believe that by next year (2017), cash payments will account for only 23 percent of all transactions. And when people use electronic payment methods, they typically spend more than when they use cash.

In other words, if you own a food business and only accept cash, you're missing out on a lot of business.

Whether you sell your goods at bridal fairs, home parties, farmer's markets, person to person, or from your home, you'll need to have a good mobile payment set up. (Keep in mind that if you sell online, your website will act as your payment processer.)

Here are some of the best and most highly rated mobile payment processors out there.

- Square. If you're looking for simplicity in set up and ease of use, Square may be the perfect match. There are no set up fees or upfront costs, and users say it's one of the easiest to use.

With it, you'll be able to accept all credit cards, MasterCard, Visa, Discover, and American Express, and pay only 2.75 percent per swipe on all of them. The reader allows you swipe cards, read chips or perform contactless transactions. Then the funds will be transferred to your bank within 1-2 business days. To set it up, sign up at the site and give them your address so they can mail you the free reader, and then connect to your bank account. When a customer wants to pay with a credit card, open the app on your phone, plug in the reader and complete the transaction. How easy is that?

- PayAnywhere. Another simple app that is less expensive than Square. This app and reader is free, and only charges $2.69 per swipe. It allows you to accept all credit cards, including PayPal cards, and doesn't require monthly contracts or sign up charges. It works on iPhones and Androids. The company offers next day funding on your transactions.

- Intuit GoPayment. You can use this app on your Android, iPhone or iPad, and although there are monthly fees starting at $19.95, the swipe fee is lower—at just 1.6 percent. They also offer a free monthly service that offers swipe fees as low as $2.40 per swipe plus a .25 cent transaction fee.

Photographs

This is one area where you can't skimp. Your customers will buy with their eyes, and if you don't have professional photographs on your website that makes their mouths water, you probably won't get the sale. The good news is that it doesn't take a lot of money to hire a professional food photographer to get you those photos. If you look locally, you should be able to hire one for about $50 per shot. It will be a large upfront investment, but one that will pay off in sales.

A Word about Funding

Although the investment for a food business isn't large, if you don't already have your equipment, it can quickly add up. Some food business owners need a little extra help to get their business off the ground and look to outside lenders for that help. The lending environment for small businesses isn't good right now, but luckily there are other methods for getting the funding you might need. Here are some options.

- **Friends and family**. This is the most common method used for solopreneurs who need a little extra cash to get started. But if you do borrow from your family or friends, I recommend that you keep it on the up and up and create a legal contract with the repayment terms clearly spelled out. Otherwise, doing business with those you love could put a strain on your relationship.

- **Alternative lenders.** Because the banks have reduced loans to small businesses, other types of lenders have stepped in to fill the gap. Called alternative lenders, these lenders offer loans to people who may not be able to qualify for a bank loan. But caution is advised because the interest rates and repayment terms on these types of loans can be steep. And if all your profits are going toward high interest rates, it will take much longer for your business to support you. Some of the most popular alternative lenders for small loans are Prosper.com. LendingClub.com, Accion.org, and OpportunityFund.org.

- **Crowdfunding.** Crowdfunding sites like KickStarter.com and IdieGoGo.com allow you put up your business idea and ask people to fund it for you in return for gifts and perks. These sites can be a great way to raise money if you have the ability to put together an attractive package that makes people want to fund you.

And that, believe it or not, is all the equipment you'll need to start your own home-based food business. Not a lot, is it? Of course, I didn't mention the obvious things like the phone you'll need to take customer orders and accept credit card payments and the computer you'll need to run your website, but you probably already have those things.

Isn't it amazing that you can build a successful business on so little? Just think, some kitchen equipment that you probably already have, an automobile, which you also likely have, an easy-to-do website and a free mobile payment app and you're on your way to food business bliss.

Do you think if everyone knew how easy it was to set up a food business, they'd be doing it too? Don't worry, it'll be our little secret.

Now, are you ready for the next chapter? In it, we'll talk about how to source products and find them at the best price. Ready? Let's continue building your dream.

Food Business Secret Ingredient No. 4: Proper Organization Can Increase Your Profits

If you build your business using the steps I outline in this book in the same order, you will be able to increase your profits. How? Because an organized business is an efficient one, and when you run a business that requires your time, like a food business, time is money. But if you're organized and keep to your system, you will be able to reduce the amount of time you put into it, which will increase your profits. So stay on track and don't try and rush ahead by skipping any of the important steps I outline in this book.

CHAPTER SIX:

How to Buy Ingredients and Packaging at Wholesale Prices (And Where to Find Them)

Can you believe that we're about halfway there? In a few more chapters, you'll have all the information you'll need to begin down the path of starting and running a home-based food business.

Exciting, isn't it?

But before you can prepare, package and sell your products, you'll need to source them. After all, you can't just walk into a grocery store and purchase items off the shelf to make your foods—not if you want to make a profit that will support your business.

But before we take a look at some of the places you can use to source your ingredients at a bulk or wholesale price, let's talk about why it's so important.

When totaling your sales at the end of every month, you'll calculate your gross sales and net profit. Your net profit is what you'll need to concentrate on because it tells you what your actual profit is after deducing all of your expenses. Here's an example of what that looks like for cupcake business.

Gross sales (a total of all the sales made for the month) $3,500

Expenses (this is a calculation of all your expenses, including, ingredients, equipment amortization, your time, and transportation expenses) $1,500

Net Profit (This is your gross sales minus your expenses) $2,000

Now, the goal is to make your net profit as high as you can because that's the amount of money you truly earn in your business. And how can you do that? By reducing your expenses.

Raw ingredients are one of the biggest expenses in a food business, but if you shop correctly, you can reduce those expenses significantly. (In a future chapter, I'll outline step-by-step how to price your products and then teach you how to figure out what it cost you to make them.)

The price you pay for your ingredients all depends on where you buy them. Here is some guidance on where to get the best deals.

Where to Source Your Food Ingredients

The place where you purchase your raw ingredients from will all depend on what you plan to sell. And because cottage foods can be so diverse, I've compiled a list of all the possible bulk or wholesale food sources below. Be sure to research each one to determine which type of seller is right for you.

Restaurant Supply Shops. These types of stores sell at a wholesale level to restaurants and other food vendors. In them, you can find commercial equipment (think mixers at wholesale prices for you bakers!), and some bulk foods. For example, if you need to purchase flour, sugar, butter, and some fruits in bulk, this might be the place to do it. You'll also find various cans, jars, and other packaging options. You can find these stores in most major cities, or visit online restaurant supply sites like the WebstaurantStore.

Bakery Supply Stores. If you're planning to sell baked goods, you should definitely check out the local bakery supply stores in your area. These stores carry everything you need at bulk prices including, flour, sugar, icing, fondant, and decorations. You'll also find pans, cupcake tins and holders, cake boxes, pastry boxes and inserts, and just about everything you'll need to prepare your food. Keep in mind that when you're purchasing 50 pound flour and sugar bags, you'll likely get a better price locally because you won't have to pay for shipping. But if you want to explore the online possibilities, or if you don't have a local shop, check out PastryChef.com, KitchenKrafts.com, and BakeDeco.com.

Canning Supply Stores. If you're going to can vegetables, jams, sauces or other mouthwatering foods, then you'll need a good supplier for your jars, lids and other equipment. KitchenKrafts.com offers a great selection, as does Freund Container and Supply, and AllAmericanCanner.com, which offers jars by the pallet. When communicating with these companies, be sure to let them know that you are interested in bulk or wholesale pricing.

Wholesale Nuts. If you're going to sell spiced or flavored nuts, you'll need a great wholesale supplier because nut prices are expensive. You can sometimes find them at local restaurant supply stores, or online at sites like IFSBulk.com, Nuts.com, or NutStop.com. Again, the prices advertised aren't always the wholesale prices, so be sure to ask.

Vegetables. If you're going to can fresh vegetables or fruits, you'll need a source of fresh produce, and you're most likely to find that in your local area. Your best bet is to seek out local farms and talk to them about buying produce in bulk or at a wholesale price. If you don't have local farms in your area, go to the nearest farmer's market and talk to the vendors about making the same kind of deal. And if you have the space, many food producers grow their own. This drastically reduces expenses and increases that ever important net profit.

Use a Sales Tax Permit to Place Your Orders

Keep in mind that in order to purchase your ingredients on a wholesale level, you'll likely need a sales tax permit. This will also prevent you from having to pay sales tax on the purchase because you can present the seller with an exemption, which means you're purchasing the product for your business. To get your sales tax number, contact your local Department of Revenue or Comptroller's office. The IRS publishes a handy list called State Government Websites, and it provides links to every state government office so you can find yours.

Where to Source Your Packaging Materials

Nothing sells an artesian food products more than packaging, but unless you buy yours right, it could put a serious dent in your profits. You'll definitely want to purchase your packaging materials in bulk or at wholesale pricing so you will earn as much profit as possible in your business.

Here's a list of great places where you can find just about every type of packaging you'll need.

- **Pouches.** If your product will fit in a stand up pouch, check out StandUpPouches.net. These pouches will work for cookies, nuts, popcorn, and dry mixes.

- **Bags.** Clear bags work for many different types of foods, including candy, nuts, cookies, pastries and breads. ClearBags.com offers cone shaped, square, and flat bags—in other words, you can find just about any type of clear bag you need at this site.

- **Plastic containers.** If you sell drinks or cupcakes and want clear plastic containers, Cuptainers.com is the place to get them at great wholesale prices.

- **Decorative packaging.** If your style is a little more elaborate and you want fancy cake boxes, specialty ribbons, and other fanciful containers, PaperMart.com is a great place to find all of that and more. To create stickers, brochures and other paper-type packaging take a look at PSPrint.com. (Remember, you'll have to adhere to your state's labeling laws for all your food products, and a sticker is a great way to do that.)

- **Miscellaneous packaging.** If you're looking for something out of the ordinary like hot drink throwaway cups, entre containers, plastic soup bowls with lids, green packaging, and even custom packaging, look no further than FoodPackagingWarehouse.com. You'll find tons of ideas and selections for your business.

- **Bakery bags and shipping supplies.** Uline.com offers a wide assortment of bakery bags for every shape and size of bread or pastry you make. The site also offers a great selection of corrugated boxes, bubble wrap and other shipping supplies if you decide to sell your products online.

- **Bottles.** If you need wholesale plastic or glass bottles or jars, ebottles.com is a great place to look. They have a wide variety and prices that are difficult to match. Containerandpackaging.com is another great resource.

Also, you can find great packaging options at your local restaurant supply and bakery supply stores, but you won't always find the low prices that you do at online wholesalers, even after you pay shipping. Be sure to look closely at all your options so you'll earn the highest profit possible.

And finally, don't forget to provide your sales tax number when you purchase your packaging supplies because it will keep you from having to pay sales tax.

Food Business Secret Ingredient No. 5: Pay Attention to Your Bottom Line

You'll put a lot of work into your home-based food business, and it's only fair that you earn a profit large enough to make it worthwhile. Keep in mind that for every penny you save on your expenses, that's a penny in your pocket—and they can add up. For instance, imagine that you sourced flour for less and it amounted to .10 cents less per cupcake. If you sold 1,000 cupcakes per month, you would earn an additional $100 per month. Now just think how much extra you could earn if you made small budget tweaks like that on every expense?

CHAPTER SEVEN:

How to Price Your Product for Sales AND Profit

With all the exciting talk of designing and branding your food business, it's easy to forget about one important aspect: making money. Yes, you probably have a passion for baking or canning or cake decorating, but let's be honest: you're going to put many hours into your food business, and it's only fair that you're well compensated for it. Otherwise, you could use your talent to prepare your foods for your family, friends, or even your church functions.

But when you're baking for your business, you need to be smart about how much you charge so you can turn a profit.

People approach this in many ways, but I'm going to lay out what I've found to be the most logical system. First, you'll need to estimate your expenses, and then we'll go from there.

How to Estimate Your Expenses

In your food business, you'll have fixed and variable costs. Fixed expenses are those that stay stagnant and don't change. For instance, the cost of your equipment and displays that you purchase when starting your business is a fixed expense. As is the rent you pay on your booth at the farmer's market. Total those up and put them in a fixed expenses column, either in a notebook or using a spreadsheet.

For instance, if you spent $2,000 on equipment and displays and pay $35 every month for a booth at your local farmer's market, you'll have to take those expenses into account before you can count a profit. Your first $2,000 in sales will go toward the equipment and displays costs, and can't be counted as profit. And once you've paid for that, the first $35 in sales every month will go toward your booth and can't be counted as profit.

In other words, in the beginning of your business you'll use every bit of your initial gross profits to pay back the fixed expenses before you can count a net profit.

How to Figure Variable Expenses

Now things get a little trickier. You'll need to figure your variable expenses, which mostly include your raw ingredients and packaging. For this example, I'm going to use a cupcake business. You would need to figure the amount of each ingredient that it takes to make a batch of cupcakes.

For this example, I'll use some rounded numbers that make it easy, but you can figure your own ingredient expenses using the same formula, based on how much you pay and which ingredients you use.

For this example, I'll use 5 pound bags of flour and sugar.

---

5 pound bag of flour (20 cups) = $4.00
5 pound bag of sugar (10 cups) = $4.00
4 sticks of butter = $4.00

Imagine that to make your cupcakes, you would use 2 cups of flour, 1 cup of sugar and 2 sticks of butter. The raw ingredients for your recipe would cost:

Flour: 2 cups = .20 cents
Sugar: 1 cup = .40 cents
Butter: 2 sticks = $2

So, your ingredients for a batch of 12 cupcakes would cost $2.60. Obviously, you would also need to figure the costs for your frosting, packaging, and decorations by following the same formula, but for this example, we'll keep it simple.

But we're not finished.

Next, you'll need to figure in your time and labor. Many newbie food business owners leave this part out of the equation, but trust me, that would be a mistake. The amount of time you put into sourcing your ingredients, producing them, marketing them, and transporting them should all be reimbursed. The question is, how much will you pay yourself?

There are many schools of thought about this, and some new business owners don't pay themselves in the beginning because they choose to put all profits back into the business to help it grow, but you'll still need a number in order to judge how profitable your business is.

Let's imagine that you decide on $15 per hour and you're baking and delivering 1 batch of cupcakes. You would figure your labor costs this way:

Time to bake and decorate 1 batch: 1 hour
Time to deliver: 1 hour

So, for that batch, your labor cost would be $30.00. Next, you'll add that $30.00 to the cost of ingredients, ($2.60) to come up with 32.60.

Let's summarize:

Your total costs for creating 1 batch of 12 cupcakes is $32.60. If you sold them for $3 each, your net profit would be $3.40. That may not sound like a lot, but what if you sold 1,500 cupcakes a month? (Completely doable.) In that case, the net profit for your business would be $566, and you would personally be paid $2,500 for your labor expenses. If you raised your prices to $4 per cupcake, your profit and salary would be even more.

Now I realize that the numbers will change, depending on how your run your business. For instance, in the example above, I added a $15 labor charge for delivery, but if you're selling most of your cupcakes at one time, you wouldn't charge a $15 labor fee for every batch, but just once, which would give you more net profits. In addition, you can set a minimum order and that will help keep your costs down.

And if you want more of a salary and less to put into the business, you can increase your labor costs. Just keep in mind that you should keep some of the money in your business in order to restock raw ingredients, packaging, and to market your business.

Here it is in a nutshell: you should figure your costs, then settle on how much you want to earn every month and work backwards from there. For instance, if your goal is to only earn $1,000 a month, you would figure the cost of your ingredients, packaging, and labor costs and work it backwards to determine how many cupcakes you need to sell. And if you want to earn more, simply increase the amount of cupcakes you sell until you reach your desired amount.

It's really not as hard as it sounds, and once you've got it down, it will come as second nature to you. And to make it even easier, MoneySavingMom.com offers a free downloadable recipe cost calculator spreadsheet you can use to figure the costs on all your recipes.

How are you doing? Can you imagine your food business? Is it coming to life in your head? I hope so because next we're going to talk about something very important: where to sell your home produced goods.

Food Business Secret Ingredient No. 6: Price Your Goods Competitively

No matter how good your artesian bread is, if it's not priced competitively, you may not get the sales you need to stay profitable. If after figuring your costs, you can't be competitive and still make a profit, you will either have to change your ingredients or buy them cheaper, or pay yourself a lower hourly wage. If neither of these are an option, you may need to work on promoting your brand as higher quality to make customers feel good about paying a higher price.

CHAPTER EIGHT

Where Will You Sell Your Homemade Foods?

Okay, let's take stock. You've decided on a food that you will make in your kitchen and sell to the public. You've created your own unique brand and story that will draw customers to you. You've found your ideal sources for ingredients and packaging, and you understand how to price your products so you will earn a good profit. What's next?

Only one of the most important decisions you'll make in this process: where to sell your food.

Remember, every state has cottage food laws that dictate where home-based food producers can sell their products, so it's important to check chapter ten to find out what your options are. I'll go over each option in this chapter so you'll have a good idea of where you want to sell yours.

Famers Markets and
Other Outdoor Venues

Many people in this type of business sell their products at farmers markets, fairs, music concerts, sporting events, or expos for a very good reason: it's where people go to find local food. In fact, it's been a starting place for many national brands such as Justin's nut butters. But it's not as easy as just setting up a booth at your local market. It takes some forethought and a plan to get it right. Here's a general outline of how to successfully sell your products at your local farmer's market.

- **Find the Right Market.** You may only have one market in your area, or you may have several to choose from. Visit each one and look at the visitors to determine which market is right for your product. You'll also want to ensure that there aren't too many other vendors who already sell what you plan to. You can check LocalHarvest.org to find all the markets in your area.

- **Check with the Market Manager.** Before you consider selling at a particular market, you'll need to check with the market manager to first determine if there is booth space, and then ask if selling your product is permissible. Some markets limit the number of similar food vendors, and others offer exclusivity. In that case, if there is already a cupcake vendor, your request may not be approved. You should also ask about the fees to determine whether or not they're affordable. Managers may ask you for a picture of your product and/or booth, what you will sell and for copies of your license and tax information.

- **Consider Insurance.** Many farmer's markets require vendors to have product liability insurance in case a customer is sick or injured by the food. Check with yours to determine if this is a requirement. Keep in mind that even if it's not required, it's a good idea to have it.

- **Think about the Weather.** Some locations, like Arizona and Texas, have melting heat in the summer that makes it difficult for some fresh food vendors. For example, cupcake icing has a tendency to melt in that kind of weather. In addition to using the special melt-proof icing I suggested in the recipe section of this book, you can also use "fake" cupcakes as displays or place your products on gel packs to help them keep cool. You can also keep the majority of your perishable goods in a cooler, and then replace them on your table as they sell.

- **Have Enough Change.** Even though many people will use their debit or credit cards to make a purchase, some people will use cash so it's important that you take enough small bills to make change.

- **Take Along a Friend.** When the crowd hits, it will be difficult for just one person to keep up. At least until you're familiar with the process, take along a friend to help you keep up.

- **Know What's Hot.** Foodies like to keep up with what's hot in the food world, and are more likely to purchase homemade foods made by vendors who also keep up with trends. For instance, gluten free foods are popular, as are low sugar jams, cupcakes with a healthy twist, and artesian breads made with organic ingredients.

- **Sell Add-On Products.** One of the ways to increase your income when selling at farmer's markets is to increase your offering. For example, if you sell bread, consider also canning and selling jams, nut butters, or savory relishes. If you sell cupcakes, have a custom cake display on site where customers can special order them.

- **Think "To-Go" Foods**. Most of the time, people who shop farmer's markets don't want to buy an entire pie and lug it around the market. Instead, they're looking for quick bites of food, or foods that they can take home and enjoy later without a lot of hassle. Homemade canned goods, cupcakes in singles or 6-packs, nuts, popcorn, and sauces are products that do well in these types of venues. If you make pies and cakes and want to sell those, reduce them to hand pies or slices of cake and you'll do better. (But be sure to let customers know that you take custom orders.)

- **Partner with Other Vendors.** In these days of social media, it's easy to partner with other vendors who sell complimentary products in order to increase sales. For instance, at my local market last year, the goat cheese guy and the woman who sold peaches partnered and told customers about a recipe using both ingredients. It definitely increased both vendor's sales. Take a look around your market and determine which vendor would make a good partner for you, and then once you form a partnership, use your social media accounts to let customers know about it.

- **Dress the Part**. Everything you do to further your brand at the market will solidify it in customer's minds. (It's why I wear my Real Men Bake Brownies" tee-shirt.) If you bake old fashioned pies, consider wearing a vintage apron over your clothes. Or if you sell bar-b-que sauce, why not dress the part by wearing jeans and a cowboy hat? Use your imagination—the clothes you choose to wear will help bring your business' "story" to life.

- **Offer a Sign-Up Sheet.** You'll need to build a base of loyal customers, and one of the best ways to do that is by creating an email mailing list. With it, you can inform customers in advance about the flavors and new products you bring to market each week, and offer discounts and sales. Keep a sign-up sheet on your table and encourage your customers to sign up for future deals and information.

- **Catch the Kid's Attention.** If you can draw the kids toward your booth, they'll likely bring their parents—and their wallets. Use your imagination and think of something your product offers that would be of interest to kids. For example, if you sell cupcakes, you might offer a "decorate your own," cupcake stand.

- **Offer Deals of the Day.** Another way to ensure your success at the farmer's market is to offer customers a choice on pricing. For example, if they order more, they get a discount. People pay $3 per brownie at my stand, but if they order 2, they get them for $5. Be sure to take your costs into consideration before settling on price deals. You can also use this concept as the market is nearing closing time. If your food is perishable, you're better off selling it at a reduced price than taking it home only to have to throw it out. Before closing, offer a 2 for 1 sale, or another similar pricing tactic.

- **Ask for Feedback.** As a home-based food seller, you'll always want to talk to your customers and ask them for feedback. This will allow you continually improve your product or offerings and stay current on the needs of your local community. You can put a "suggestions" or "feedback" box on your table, or simply talk to them and ask questions.

- **Trade Your Leftover Product.** If you have a product that is perishable like popcorn or baked goods, you don't have to throw away the ones that didn't sell. Instead, at the end of the market, ask other vendors if they want to trade. Who knows? You could score enough fresh vegetables for the week in trade for a few dozen cupcakes.

How to Create the Perfect Farmer's Market Display

When you walk into a retail store, the way it's laid out is what likely causes you to look at certain products, or even make a purchase. It's no different with a farmer's market booth. Because there are so many things to consider, I've included a special section below to help you create your best display.

There is an art to display, and if you're going to successfully sell your product at a farmer's market (or any other venue where you're selling from a booth), you'll need to master it. Here is a list of nine things you should pay attention to when setting up your display booth.

- Your booth will likely be small, so you should display as much product as possible without making the space look too crowded.

- Put out enough stock to make it look like you have a lot to offer, and leave the rest of it in coolers or boxes underneath the table. (Cover the table with a tablecloth so customers can't see the mess underneath.)

- Put the largest product at the rear of the table, and the smaller items closer to the front.

- Offer samples, but do so in a neat and orderly way. For example, if you sell artesian cheese, cube it and put it in a covered dish with clean toothpicks nearby. My brownies are cut into neat little squares, and I also offer toothpicks to keep the sampling area sanitized. Remember, if your samples are too big or elaborately decorated, it may be enough to satisfy tasters and prevent them from buying.

- Use photos for customer orders, such as cakes or pies, but also have them on hand for other products. This works well if you run out of a certain product because it may cause someone to place an order for the next week. Imagine that you sold canned peach cobbler, but just sold your last jar. If the next customer in line was able to look at a photograph of its yummy goodness, they may place an advanced order.

- Get creative with your display. For instance, if you sell rosewater cupcakes, you can scatter fresh rose petals or rose stems on the table. If carrot cake is your specialty, why not have fresh bunches of carrots lying around?

- Be sure to slant your boxes or crates up so people can see inside them from a distance. And if you use a bakery display, use one that opens from the rear. If you're the only person in and out of the display, it will stay clean and customers will perceive it as more sanitary.

- Post signs about the products you have to offer and their prices.

- Keep your booth simple with clean lines and contrasting colors. It will you're your booth appear eye-catching and inviting.

Remember, all of the above tips can be used to successfully sell at farmer's markets, fairs, nonprofit events, and any other outdoor location your state allows you sell in. The great thing about selling in these types of locations is that you can do it in a way that best fits your own schedule. For example, if you want to set up weekly at your famer's market, you can, but if you prefer to find an event that only takes place once a month, that's an option, too.

Now, if you're prefer to sell your homemade goods online, we'll discuss that in the next section.

Online Food Business

If you'd rather not deal with customers face to face, an online food business may be a better option for you. In this type of business, you would do everything from home and simply send out your creations to people who order them online.

You have a few options when it comes to setting up an online food business. But before I get into them, I want to encourage you again to check the chapter ten to ensure that you're allowed to sell your products online. (I know, I sound like a broken record, but trust me, it would be horrible to get excited about an online cupcake business only to learn that your state won't allow it.)

One thing you should realize is that if you run a cottage food business out of your home, you will only be allowed to sell your products to customers in your state, and there are many different state rules that regulate this. For example, Washington State allows people to sell cottage foods online, but they aren't allowed to ship them—they must be picked up by the customer or delivered by the vendor. California has the same rules, but it allows customers from other states to order from you as long as they pick up the order in California. Georgia's laws are much the same. Some states like Texas, allow cottage food vendors to have a website, but don't allow any sales to take place on it.

If you want to create a nationwide food business that sells across state lines, you'll have to get your commercial food license. We'll talk about the steps you'll need to take for this type of business in chapter nine.

But for now, if you live in a state that allows you to sell online within the state, here's how to go about it.

Ask Yourself Some Questions

Before you decide to take your product online, there are some questions you'll need to ask yourself in order to decide whether or not it will be a success. Answering these questions will help you get a good idea of exactly what benefits your product will offer to potential customers.

- **Do you offer something that consumers can't buy at their local grocery store?** This is important because if they can, they may not want to pay shipping or wait for delivery.

- **Will consumers want to order your product over and over again, or is it a one-time purchase item?** If you can't rely on repeat sales, it would be difficult to build a successful online business.

- **Will your product ship easily and inexpensively?** I saw a $300 cake advertised on Amazon that was 12 inches high. I can't image how the seller will get it in one piece to buyers. What about your product? Is it feasible to ship it safety and affordably?

- **Does your product make a good gift or is it only for self-consumption?** Think of Shari's Berries—people all over the nation send them out as gifts, and she has been very successful in her business. If your product makes a great gift, it will only increase your chances for success. Remember, if your product will be given as a gift, you'll need to pay special attention to the packaging. The recipient should feel as if they're opening a present.

If you've seriously considered these questions and still feel that your product would do well online, here are the steps you should take to get started.

Create an Online Presence

Your first step in the process is to create an online presence so that hungry customers can find you. We talked about how to set up a website in a previous chapter, and if you plan to sell online, you'll need to make sure your site allows customers to order and pay online.

But if you want to get the most out of your website, you'll need to let people know it's there. And the best way to do that is to market your online business.

How to Market Your Online Food Business

Even if your state won't allow you to ship your products to customers, you can still use a website to increase your business. Customers can place orders online, even if you aren't allowed to collect payments from them. Here are a couple of ways to market your site to increase your home-based food business.

- **Display your website address at all events.** Wherever you set up and sell your products, you should prominently display your website address so customers can find you online. You can include it on your signage, in brochures, pamphlets, business cards, and on your product labels. Be sure to let customers know that you announce your flavors, designs, specials, and discounts on your site so they'll visit frequently.

- **Use it to take advanced orders.** What happens if you sell out of your sought after organic bone broth at the local farmer's market? If you don't have a website, you would have to simply take a loss on sales and hope that the customers would come back the next week, but if you have one, you can use it to take orders and continue selling right there at the booth using a smartphone or tablet. Customers can place orders, and if you're allowed to ship, they'll receive the product in a few days—a much shorter wait than if they had to wait until the next market day. Even if you're not allowed to ship, you can still make the sale and deliver the product the next week.

- **Use your website to upsell.** Imagine that you sell hand pies at a local farmer's market, but also offer beautifully made full size sweet potato pies. In addition to having a pie on hand at the market to show off your baking skills, you can also pull up your website and show tempting photos of your pies. Then, customers can place custom orders right then and there.

- **Use local SEO to draw new customers.** The people in your area are likely looking for the very products you make, and would prefer to buy them from a home baker so they'll know where the ingredients came from and who made them. That's why you should use local SEO tactics to draw in local customers when they search online for local food products.

- **Use social media.** No business can survive in today's culture without a solid social media plan. Consumers eat with their eyes, so food business owners have a perfect opportunity to reach out to consumers with expertly taken photos of their products. Instagram and Pinterest are two examples of social media platforms that can be used to whet the appetites of consumers. In addition, Neeach.com is a foodie social media platform that every food entrepreneur should be on!

An online presence can really up your game in a local market, so it's important that you tell all your customers about your site. And remember, just because your state may not allow you to collect payments or ship in state this year, that doesn't mean it won't change. Cottage food laws are constantly changing as more and more consumers demand it and lawmakers realize that the practice truly doesn't pose a threat to the public.

But if you want to take it a step further, you'll need to get your commercial food license. I'll tell you how to do that in chapter nine, and once you do it, you'll be able to sell your products across state lines. Here are a few outlets to consider. I recommend that you use as many of them as possible in order to reach more customers.

- **Etsy.** If you want a virtual store that already has traffic, Etsy is a great place to set up shop. Although you will lose a percentage of your sale to fees, the built-in traffic is worth the cost. Etsy's rules for selling homemade food in their store is that you comply with your state laws. In other words, if you're allowed to sell online, then as long as you have the required licenses, inspections, and permits, you can sell there. And keep in mind that if your state doesn't allow cottage food vendors to sell online, you can expand your business to a commercial kitchen and do it that way. We'll talk more about that in a later chapter.

- **Amazon.** Amazon isn't only for books and home goods! They have a category called "grocery and gourmet foods," where individual food producers are allowed to sell their products. Once your business is licensed correctly, you can offer your products on this mega-site.

- **Direct Eats.** This site is dedicated to local producers all over the country and caters to consumers who want to buy artesian foods. It's free to list an unlimited amount of products on the site. The site pays for credit card fees and shipping, but you'll have to pay a percentage of the sale to the site.

- **CrateJoy.com.** Subscription boxes are wildly popular right now, and if your products lend themselves to a monthly subscription model, you should seriously consider it. And when you use a company like Crate Joy, you'll have all you need to set up a store on their site and begin offering subscription services. You can use your own domain name and link your Crate Joy site to your own website. Products like pastries, candy, jams, seasoned nuts and more would all make great monthly "crates." Sign up now and get a free 14 day trail and after that pay $39 per month, plus a 1.25 percent plus .10 cent transaction fee per sale.

If you'd rather concentrate on baking, preserving, or cooking your products, it's possible to hire experts to put together your website, brand, and packaging to help you sell your goods online. Ediblecommerce.com is run by a food entrepreneur and it offers newbie food sellers all that and more.

Now, let's move on to a topic that puzzles many first time online food producers: shipping.

How to Ship Perishable Food Products

If you're going to sell your food online, you've got to learn how to properly ship it or you will not only lose out on repeat business, but you find yourself refunding an inordinate amount of orders. A few years ago, I ordered a specialty ice cream kit for my father, who happens to be an ice cream fanatic. When it arrived, it was a gooey mess because the shipper hadn't properly packed it or prepared the package for the intense summer heat. I quickly called and complained and was given a refund. But my experience would have been very different if the seller had simply used some common sense when shipping their product.

If your goods aren't perishable, such as canned goods, peanuts, and popcorn, you can just ensure that they're individually packaged properly and packed in a way that won't squish it or break the glass. But if you're product is perishable, like cupcakes, brownies or other baked goods, you'll have to take some more precautions.

Here's a basic rundown on how you should approach the packaging and shipping of your perishable goods.

Determine the Correct Shipping Time

The faster shipping time you use, the more you and your customer will pay for the service, so you should put a lot of thought into this step in the process. Most vendors who sell perishable foods ship it on either an overnight or a two day delivery, depending on how well the product will hold up. (The way the product is packed plays a huge role in this—see below.)

If you can use two day shipping, your customers will likely purchase from you more often because they will have to spend less—and you can always offer overnight shipping as an upgrade. However you decide to ship your food products, make sure you spell it out on your website to avoid any problems with sales.

Some vendors use different shipping times depending on the season. For instance, in the summer, they'll ship their products overnight to avoid spoilage in the hot summer sun, but in the fall and winter, they'll use 2 day shipping. Practice shipping your products in various packaging options to determine the best materials and time for them.

In addition, you should time your shipping so that packages never sit over the weekend. If you only shop on Mondays, Tuesdays, and Wednesdays, you won't have to worry about your product going bad and having a disappointed customer.

Select the Right Carrier

You have a lot of options when it comes to which carrier you'll use for your products, but most food vendors who sell perishable foods choose either Federal Express or UPS because they can rely on the fact that the product will get to its location on time.

I suggest calling each of the carriers and talking to them about a discount rate for volume business. In your business plan, you should have created sales projections and you can use this figure when negotiating with them. Plan on getting at least a 30 percent reduction in the carrier's retail prices.

Finally, make sure that whatever carrier you use, the customer can track their package. This will give them more confidence and relieve you of the responsibility of having to do it for them and then communicating what you find out.

Pack Your Products Properly

Remember the specialty ice cream kit fiasco? You'll need to avoid something like that from happening at all costs. The best way to ensure your products arrive safe and sound is to pack them properly.

If your food items are perishable, you'll need to keep them cool or frozen on the trip to your customer's house. Here are a few options to do that:

- **Styrofoam boxes**. If you use these containers for your product, you will have to use less ice packs to keep them cool. Remember the thicker the container, the cooler it will stay. You can find Styrofoam containers, along with everything else mentioned on this list, at places like MrBoxOnline.com, Uline.com, and Freund Container and Supply.

- **Styrofoam inserts.** These are inserts that fit into standard sized boxes, or can be cut to fit any box. They won't hold the cool as well as Styrofoam boxes, but are definitely less expensive. You'll find them at the above mentioned sites.

- **Insulated liners and pads**. These products are made to wrap around your Styrofoam boxes, and many companies use them successfully. Again, use the above links to find them.

- **Ice.** Depending on whether you need to keep your product cool or frozen, you'll use either ice packs or dry ice. Ice packs will help keep your product cool, and to keep expenses down, you can purchase one time use ice packs. You will need to use an insulated or Styrofoam box in combination with ice packs. On the other hand, dry ice will help keep your products frozen. There are special rules to follow if you ship with dry ice, so be sure to contact your carrier to learn the rules before shipping. Both Federal Express and UPS offer written guidelines for dry ice use. Dryiceinfo.com offers a chart that tells you how much dry ice you'll need per pound of product and time in transit.

What if Something Goes Wrong?

Things will happen that are out of your control, and as a business owner, it will be up to you to determine how to handle it. Most experts agree that if you take the stance that the customer is always right, your business will prosper. For example, if the package was delivered and put in a place where the customer didn't see it for a day and it caused the food to go bad, you should simply resend another one. This attitude of always making sure your customers are happy and satisfied will bring in referrals and repeat business.

Okay, that sums up how to set up an online food business. Remember, if you're going to sell to customers in other states, you'll need to get your commercial food license. More on that later.

But now, let's turn back to cottage food production and talk about one of the easiest ways to make a living at it: selling directly to customers from your home.

Selling Your Food Products from Your Home

Maybe the thought of lugging hundreds of cupcakes or jars of barbeque sauce to the local market doesn't excite you. Or maybe the idea of leasing a commercial kitchen to sell your products online is more than you had in mind. Don't worry—you can always run a laid back business that is built around your time schedule and lifestyle by simply selling products from your home.

Unless you already have a built in customer base such as neighbors or friends who can't get enough of your product, this type of business model will be the slowest to build. That's because you won't be in front of consumers on a regular basis, and you'll have to rely on getting the word out about your goods before you see any business. Some businesses do better than others with this model. For instance, a custom cake decorating business could do very well if you are able to get photos and prices in front of brides to be or moms who need cakes for birthday parties. On the other hand, dried pasta, loose teas, roasted coffee, or snacks like nuts or popcorn probably wouldn't do as well.

One thing to keep in mind with this type of business is that you won't have a professional location to interact with clients at. You may have to sit at your kitchen table to help a bride decide on a cake, or meet up with a party planner at the local coffee shop. But as long as you stay professional and deliver what you promise, that shouldn't be a problem.

If you like this slower paced food business model, here are a few ideas to help get the word out about your new business.

- **Ask to speak at organizations.** There are many organizations that are always on the lookout for speakers at their events. And if you can somehow tie in your business with their topic, you'll have a captive audience who may end up buying from you. For instance, you can offer to speak at a local Mother's of Preschoolers (MOP's) meeting about how to best plan a kid's birthday party. Of course, you'll be introduced as a custom cake baker who specializes in kid's parties, and you'll probably pass out a lot of business cards and brochures.

- **Partner up.** If you're specialty is wedding cakes, why not partner with a wedding planner and give each other referrals for business? Or if you prefer to bake cakes for retirement parties, partner up with an event planner. The possibilities are endless, and the more partnerships you create, the more business will come your way.

- **Hold classes**. If your target market is the general public, why not hold your own classes to introduce yourself to the general public? You could hold a cake decorating class free of charge to showcase your skills, and hand out brochures that outline your services. Or you could teach a class about canning and homesteading if that ties in better with your product line.

- **Advertise locally.** You can also draw customers from your local area by running ads on sites like Craigslist, your town's online website, or in the local paper. If you do your research and plan correctly, you won't have to spend a lot of money on this. For instance, Craigslist is free, and many local small papers charge very little for ads run in the classifieds.

- **Word of Mouth.** Don't forget about word of mouth—it's probably the fastest way to grow your business. You can simply ask your customers to refer you to their friends and family, or you can provide them with incentives. For example, you can give them a cake in exchange for ten referrals.

We've got one more sales method to consider before we move on to talk about how to expand a cottage food business into a commercial kitchen. Next, we'll talk about how to sell your products wholesale to local specialty stores and other retailers.

Selling Your Products Wholesale

If you don't want to deal with the general public, or think you would rather deal in bulk, selling your food products wholesale might be the right path for you. Unfortunately, not all states allow cottage food vendors to sell wholesale, so be sure to check your state's laws. For instance, Texas doesn't allow cottage food producers to sell wholesale, but Iowa does, and producers in California can do it with an upgraded cottage food license.

If you can sell to retailers, you'll have to make some adjustments to both your packaging and pricing in order to cause wholesale buyers to be interested in your products. Here are a few things you need to know.

- **Stay within your borders.** If your cottage food laws allow you to sell wholesale, it means that you can only sell your products to retailers in your state. If you want to sell wholesale on a national level, you will have to get certified as a commercial kitchen just like you would if you sold your products online nationally.

- **Up Your production.** You will have to produce much more product, which means you'll need sufficient space to produce it. For example, if you sell to your local bakery, they'll likely ask you to deliver dozens of product every day.

- **You'll have to offer wholesale pricing.** You won't be able to ask retail prices for your product because the store or shop has to sell it their customers at a marketable price. When retailers buy products in bulk, they expect a wholesale price. This means you'll make less money on your product, but will sell more of it. Retailers like to add 30-50 percent on to the price they pay for goods, so you will need to lower your prices by that much. For example, using our example cupcake pricing model from our pricing chapter, if you sold 100 cupcakes a week at retail ($3 per cupcake), you would earn $300 in profit. If the retailer wanted a 30 percent discount, you would sell your cupcakes to him for $2.10 each. So, to make that same amount on a wholesale level that you would selling them retail, you would have to sell 143 cupcakes.

- **Consider your packaging.** Depending on what you sell, you may have to redesign your packaging in order to successfully wholesale your products. If you sell cupcakes to a bakery, you won't need to worry about packaging because the cakes will simply be displayed in a bakery case. But if you sell specialty nuts to a concession stand owner, they will have to be packaged in an attractive way. Be sure to account for any packaging changes in your cost estimates.

- **Think about delivery charges**. You'll have to decide whether or not to add delivery charges to your price. Most people offer free delivery within a 30 mile radius, and then tack on a charge for distances that are farther. This is especially important if you have to make deliveries to nearby towns and cities.

There are many outlets you can approach if you decide to go the wholesale route. Get to know your local area—and those surrounding you—and make a list of businesses to approach. Here's a list of possibilities to get your wheels spinning.

- If you sell baked goods such as pies, cakes, cupcakes and scones, your local bakeries are an obvious choice.

- Restaurants also buy homemade goods from sellers, and this especially true for deserts and bread products. In addition, barbeque restaurants may be interested in your sauce for both the meals they serve, or to offer it in bottles for sale.

- Caterers are another option for selling your products wholesale. If you have a unique product that can't be found elsewhere, a caterer may purchase it from you and offer it to their clients.

- Bed and breakfasts and small local hotels can also be approached. Your canned jam and jellies would fit in nicely as an add on purchase, as would fresh baked goods or quick snacks.

- Specialty shops are a great avenue for home-based food producers. I was approached by a local shop because they'd tasted one of my brownie and wanted to sell them in their store. The sky is the limit on what you can sell in these local shops, so be sure to approach them.

You shouldn't just limit yourself to one avenue, but approach and make deals with as many retailers as you can. Remember, the more you sell, the more profits you'll put in your pocket. Just be sure that you are capable of delivery for every order you take. If you over commit even one time and don't deliver, you will likely lose the account forever.

Wow—we've talked about everything you need to do in order to start a successful home-based food business. It's a lot to take in, but when you break it down and approach it in the way I've suggested in this book, you will surely build a food business that you can rely on for the income you need.

But wait—I'm sure not all of you are going to be satisfied with keeping your business at home. After all, some states limit the amount of money you can make from a cottage food business, and you may want to earn more than that. If you max out your income level, or just want to take your food business to the next level, you'll need to get a commercial food license.

How do you do that? Come on, let's talk about it in the next chapter.

Food Business Secret Ingredient No. 7: You Don't Have to Choose Just One Venue

If you're having a difficult time deciding between selling your products at the local farmer's market, from your home, online, or at the wholesale level, don't worry because you can do it all. There is no reason why you can't go to market on the weekends, fill online orders Monday through Wednesday, and drop off deliveries to that specialty shop down the street on Thursdays. A home-based food business can be as big as you want to make it. If you have the time and energy, you could grow a business that fully supports you and your family.

CHAPTER NINE:

Growing Up:
How to Take Your
Cottage Food Business
to the Next Level

So, you've developed your food business and are doing well in your local community. So well, in fact, that you think you want to take the next step and begin selling on a larger basis. You want to sell on a wholesale level and see your products on grocery store shelves everywhere.

The good news is that it's completely doable. If you decide to take your business to the next level, you will no longer rely on the cottage food laws in your state, but will be guided by the FDA.

What follows is an outline of the steps you'll need to take if you decide to grow your business and begin selling without any restrictions on size, volume, or ingredients.

Scale Your Recipe

Sure your cookies are great when cooked in your home oven, but what happens to the recipe when it's scaled up to produce mass amounts of product? It changes, that's what. The first step you'll need to take in order to go to the next level is to scale your recipe. You have a few options to accomplish this.

- **Do it yourself.** It's possible to scale your recipe up yourself, but unless you understand food science, it may not be the best option. Because food ingredients act differently when put together in larger batches, you likely won't get the same taste that you do in your home kitchen. But if you want to try it, you'll need to rent a commercial kitchen so you'll have access to commercial sized equipment. And then you'll need to tweak your recipe over and over again until you get the taste you desire. During the process, you'll need to concentrate on creating the best possible product at the lowest cost.

- **Hire an Expert.** It's possible to hire a culinary consultant or recipe developer to assist you in scaling up your recipe. These experts often work with food business owners who want to begin producing their foods commercially. Start with the Food Consultants Group, which has consultants in every state, or ORC International. You can also google "food consultants" or "recipe developer" in your state to find more options.

- **Hire a Co-Packer.** Co-packers offer a lifeline for food business owners who don't want to cook and package everything themselves. They use your recipe and packaging to produce the products for you. Many of them offer recipe scaling as a part of their service. You can find experienced food co-packers at SpecialtyFoodResource.com, ContractPackaging.com, and at PartnerSlate.com.

Learn the Federal Rules

When packaging and selling your products across state lines, you have to become familiar with the federal rules and guidelines that govern the process. For starters, you'll need different permits than cottage food producers do, but those permits depend on the type of food you plan to produce. You should contact your local Health Department to find out which types of permits are required in your area. The CDC publishes a list of all the Health Departments in the U.S.

In addition, you'll need understand and follow the FDA's Good Manufacturing Practices, which outline the safety, sanitary and production regulations every commercial food producer must follow. The FDA lists them in excruciating detail on their website.

Either you (if you rent a commercial kitchen and produce the food on your own) or your food co-packer needs to develop a Hazard Analysis and Critical Control Points (HACC) plan. This plan assures the FDA that you are adhering to the rules and your food is being produced safely. You won't be able to produce your products without one. Again, you find all the details of a HACC plan on the FDA's website.

Decide How Your Food will be Produced

We talked a little about co-packers, also called co-manufacturers, and you'll need to decide whether you want to take on all the responsibilities of manufacturing your products yourself or if you want to partner with a contract manufacturing company to do it. The three most important considerations for this decision are:

- **Time.** If you thought you worked a lot as a cottage food producer, you haven't seen anything yet. When you produce food on a massive scale, it is not only difficult, but time consuming. If you want any kind of life outside of work, you should definitely consider hiring co-packer.

- **Cost**. On the other hand, if you hire someone to produce the products for you, you will have to pay them for the service. You won't know the amount until you speak with a few and get quotes. The quotes are based on your recipes and the amount of difficulty in producing them. On the other hand, if you choose to produce the products yourself, you will have to rent a commercial kitchen or build one in your home and those costs can add up.

- **Control**. When you allow others to produce your products, you won't have the same day to day control over the outcome as you would if you produced it yourself. This shouldn't be a problem if you're selective with the co-packer you work with. (Unless you're a complete control freak!)

If you decide to produce you own foods, you'll need to do plenty of research to find the right commercial kitchen. You can start by using sites like culinaryincubator.com, which lists over 600 commercial kitchens for rent across the nation. If you don't find one you like, you can always check with the local churches, schools and restaurants because they're often willing to rent out their kitchens in their off hours.

You can also build a commercial kitchen in your home or in a separate location. Obviously, this is the most expensive method, but if you've decided that's what you want to do, you should at least look to restaurant auction sites and Craigslist to find gently used commercial equipment in order to save on expenses.

And if you plan to hire a co-packer instead, you'll have to have discussions with more than one to find a perfect fit. A co-packer literally has the success or failure of your business in its hands, so you need to do your due diligence when deciding on one.

Your first step should be to contact them and ask for a rough estimate for the production of your food. They won't be able to give you a concrete price, but you'll need to know the range before you decide to proceed further.

If you decide to proceed, they will need to sign a non-disclosure agreement. I cannot stress to you how important this is. If they don't sign one and you give them your recipe, they can simply tweak it a little bit and then claim it as their own. Don't ever provide anyone with your recipe before they sign on of these important documents. Talk to an attorney who specializes in these agreements to have one that properly protects you drawn up.

After it's signed, you can confidently turn over your recipe and they will give you the cost of producing your product. If you're in agreement, they will run a test batch of your product for you to approve. At this point, you can either approve the product or ask for adjustments.

Once it's approved, it's time to sign a contract. You should hire a good attorney who is familiar with contract manufacturing, and please don't skip this step. There are a lot of ins and outs for this type of contract, and one poorly written clause could literally put you out of business. Some of the key highlights you should be sure are in your contract are:

- **Ask for certifications.** For example, if they're not certified with Costco or any number of other major retailers, your products can't be sold there. Be sure to have them list their certifications in the contract.

- **Verify abilities.** If you need special manufacturing facilities, you'll need to verify this in the contract. For instance, gluten free is huge right now, and if a person sensitive to gluten eats it, they get sick. If you're products are gluten-free, you'll need it in your contract that they will be produced in an area that is gluten-free.

- **Production specifics.** You'll want in writing how quickly they can produce your product, and how they will handle rush orders.

- **Price.** Just because you have a quote for today, that doesn't mean the co-packer can't raise the price tomorrow. You can set boundaries in the contract about how often prices can be raised and at what percentage.

- **Spoilage.** What happens if the co-packer orders too many ingredients for your product and it sits on their shelves until it spoils? Who is responsible for it? And how about when a careless worker damages a good amount of your packaging? All of this should be spelled out in the contract.

Test Your Product

The last step you'll need to take before you take your product to market is to test it with real people. Yes, your friends and family should give their input, but they'll *want* to like your product and their feedback may reflect this. Instead, get professional by using online survey tools like SurveyMonkey. You can get in touch with willing tasters, send them a sample, and they'll give you honest feedback. If you plan to sell an item that won't ship well, advertise in your local paper for people who will agree to sit on a product tester group. In exchange for their honest opinion, they will receive free samples of your product.

Where to Sell Product

Now that your product is produced and tested, it's time to take it to market. You will have endless options when it comes to where you will distribute it, and I've listed some of the most common ones below.

- **Direct sales.** All of the options you had when you were a cottage food producer are still open to you, so you can continue taking your product to farmer's markets, expos, fairs, and even selling them directly from your home.

- **Online sales.** Even if you were allowed to sell your product online as a cottage food producer, you could only sell within your state, and many of you had to deliver in person instead of ship the products. All that changes once you become a commercial food producer. You'll now be able to sell across state lines, or even internationally if you choose. You can sell through your own website or through the online marketplaces I listed earlier. (Or all of them.)

- **Retail stores.** You now have no limits on which grocery stores or specialty shops you sell to. You can stick to small, local stores or you can attempt to get your products in large chain stores like Whole Foods, Costco, and Walmart.

- **Tasting boxes**. Monthly box subscriptions are wildly popular, and the businesses that ship them out are always on the lookout for new food products to include in their boxes. Approach them with your products and try to strike a deal.

- **Local delivery companies.** Many cities have local artesian delivery companies, and you can try and get your products included on their lists. For example, GoodEggs.com is a great company in San Francisco, while Greenling.com delivers to many cities in central Texas. Look for one in your area and see if you can get your product featured.

- **Bakeries and restaurants**. These types of businesses are always on the lookout for original foods that they can resell to their customers. You'll have to give them wholesale prices, but it can be steady business.

- **Brokers and freelance sales representatives**. If you're not great at sales, you can hire a broker or a freelance sales representative to help get your product into stores. These salespeople are used to working with the larger chains and know how to sell and negotiate with the buyers. You'll pay a commission to them—usually about 10 percent—but if you aren't good with sales, it may be worth it.

- **Distributors.** If you want a company to handle the sales and shipping, a food distributor may be right for you. They will warehouse your product and then ship it as orders come in. Be careful though—if your products aren't selling, most distributors will cancel your line quickly, leaving you with a lot of product you may or may not be able to sell on your own.

Remember, when you sell your products wholesale, you will have to give your buyers a wholesale price, which is typically between 30 and 50 percent of the retail price. Don't forget to add shipping and delivery charges to their total price.

If you have any questions that I haven't answered, the FDA has a website that is full of helpful information for commercial food producers.

Well folks, that's about everything you need to know about making and selling products for a food business. Whether you decide to stay small in a cottage food business or stretch your wings in a commercial kitchen business, you'll have to work hard, buy smart, and sell your products with confidence. But you can do it. After all, most foodies have cooked for friends and family for years, and need some other outlet for their talents. So why not start a food business and make some extra income in the process?

If you haven't already done it, be sure to check out the next chapter where I list the cottage food laws for every state in the union.

CHAPTER TEN:

Cottage Food Laws
State by State

In order to create the perfect plan for your home-based food business, you need to understand the laws regarding cottage food production in your state. I have researched them thoroughly, and included them below for each state.

Please keep in mind that these laws change frequently, and I will do my absolute best to keep up with them and change the information in this chapter as new laws are put on the books. BUT, if I miss one, please email me at samkernsbooks@gmail.com, or get in touch with me via my website at RainMakerPress.com and let me know about it.

Thank you so much, and I hope you find that you live in a state with great laws!

Cottage Food Laws

Alabama

Certifications: Vendors must take a food safety training course

Maximum allowable income: $20,000

Approved foods: baked goods, canned jams and jellied, dried herbs or herb mix

Approved venues: farmer's markets, home, events, and roadside stands

For more information:
http://www.adph.org/ALPHTN/assets/081214Fenn.pdf

Alaska

Certifications: none required

Maximum allowable income: $25,000

Approved foods: non-potentially hazardous foods, including many not allowed in other states. If a food does not require refrigeration, it will likely be approved.

Approved venues: farmer's markets, home, events, and roadside stands

For more information:
http://dec.alaska.gov/eh/fss/food/Docs/broch_Cottage_Food.pdf

Note: some municipalities in Alaska abide by different rules, so double check with yours before you begin your business.

Arizona

Certifications: Vendors must register their business and get a food handler card.

Maximum allowable income: Unlimited

Approved foods: bread, pastries, candy, and snacks like popcorn, kettle corn, granola, crackers and pretzels.

Approved venues: farmer's markets, home, events, roadside stands, online, restaurants, retail stores

For more information:
http://www.azdhs.gov/preparedness/epidemiology-disease-control/food-safety-environmental-services/home-baked-confectionary-goods/index.php

Note: Maricopa county has tighter restrictions on selling to restaurants than the rest of the state, so if you live in that county, be sure to contact them.

Arkansas

Certifications: none required

Maximum allowable income: none

Approved foods: baked goods, candies, fruit butter, jams and jellies, honey, maple sryup

Approved venues: farmer's markets, homes, special events such as fairs and special events.

For more information:
http://www.healthy.arkansas.gov/programsservices/environmentalhealth/foodprotection/documents/cottagefoodguidelines.pdf

California

This state has two different types of licenses: Class A and Class B. Class A can only sell directly to consumers while Class B can sell to resellers.

Certifications: registration and Class A or Class B permit

Maximum allowable income: $50,000

Approved foods: baked goods, candies, popcorn products, jam and jellies, fruit butters, dry goods such as cereals and granola, breads, condiments such as honey, syrups, nut butters, and mustard, pastas, candied apples, marshmallows, spices and spice blends, chocolate covered items, nuts, crackers, pretzels, vegetable chips and more.

Approved venues: farmer's markets, home, events, roadside stands, online, restaurants, and stores.

For more information:
http://www.cdph.ca.gov/programs/pages/fdbcottagefood.aspx

Note: Not all counties allow vendors to ship their products.

Colorado

Certifications: none required

Maximum allowable income: This state limits sales to $10,000 per food item, but doesn't have an overall limit.

Approved foods: spices, teas, dehydrated produce, nuts, seeds, honey, jams and jellies, preserves, fruit butters, baked goods, candies, fruit empanadas, tortillas, and pickled vegetables that have an equilibrium PH value of 4.6 or lower.

Approved venues: farmer's markets, home, events, online

For more information:
https://www.colorado.gov/pacific/cdphe/cottage-foods-act

Connecticut

As of now, only farmers can sell their products to the general public, but there is a new that is yet to be clarified and entered. You can stay updated on the progress of the new law on this Facebook page: https://www.facebook.com/CottageFoodLawCtMovement

More information about the new law here:
https://www.cga.ct.gov/2015/ACT/PA/2015PA-00076-R00HB-05027-PA.htm

Delaware

This is another state that only allows farmers to sell homemade foods directly to consumers. You can follow the progress of the activists who are trying to change the laws here:
https://www.facebook.com/groups/1432938716947054/

More information here:
http://dda.delaware.gov/foodprod/food_processing_safety/food_processing_regs.pdf

District of Columbia

Certifications: The business must register with the state and get a permit

Maximum allowable income: $25,000

Approved foods: baked goods, candies, chocolate covered nuts and dried fruit, crackers, dried pasta, dried baking mixes, granola, cereals, herbs, sweet sorghum syrup, jams, jellies, preserves, nuts, nut butters, popcorn, grains, seeds, beans, vinegar and mustard, roasted coffee, dried tea, waffle cones, and pizzeles.

Approved venues: farmer's markets and events

More information:
http://doh.dc.gov/sites/default/files/dc/sites/doh/pu blication/attachments/New%20DOH%20Guidance% 20For%20Farmer's%20Market.pdf

Florida

Certifications: none required

Maximum allowable income: $15,000

Approved foods: breads, baked goods, candies, honey, jams, jellies, preserves, fruit pies, dried fruit, dry herbs, seasonings and mixtures, homemade pasta, cereals, granola, trail mixes, coated or uncoated nuts, vinegars, flavored vinegars, popcorn, popcorn balls.

Approved venues: farmer's markets, flea markets, roadside stands

More information:
http://www.freshfromflorida.com/Divisions-Offices/ Food-Safety/Business-Services/Food-Establishment-Inspections/Cottage-Foods

Georgia

Certifications: must be licensed, complete a training course and have your home inspected.

Maximum allowable income: No limit.

Approved foods: breads, baked goods, jams, jellies, preserves, dried fruits, herbs, seasonings and mixtures, cereals, trail mixes, granola, coated or uncoated nuts, vinegar, flavored vinegar, popcorn, popcorn balls, cotton candy.

Approved venues: non-profit events, farmer's markets, online

More information: http://agr.georgia.gov/cottage-foods.aspx

Hawaii

This state does not currently have a cottage food law, but there is one under consideration. You can read about it here:
http://www.capitol.hawaii.gov/Archives/measure_indiv_Archives.aspx?billtype=SB&billnumber=379&year=2015

Idaho

Although the state has allowed home producers to sell their products directly to consumers for year, it is just now creating a law that will clarify the guidelines. You can get more information about the possible upcoming law here: http://healthandwelfare.idaho.gov/Portals/0/Health/FoodProtection/Cottage%20Food%20Presentation.pdf?ver=2015-04-24-134932-063

Illinois

Certifications: Must register with the local county public health department and hold a current food service sanitation management certificate.

Maximum allowable income: $36,000

Approved foods: jams, jellies, preserves, fruit butters, dry herbs, tea blends, and baked goods.

Approved venues: farmer's markets, farm stands, CSA's or from a farm.

More information:
http://newillinoisfarmers.org/pdf/092015illinois_cottage_food_law.pdf

Indiana

Certifications: None required.

Maximum allowable income: No limit

Approved foods: non-potentially hazardous baked goods, fruits and vegetables, canned fruits and other foods (The PH level in these must be under 4.6 and verified before you can sell them), syrups, nuts, beans, candies, confections. The states rules are very strict on what constitutes a non-potentially hazardous food. See the link below for all the guidelines.

Approved venues: farmer's markets, roadside stands

More information:
https://www.extension.purdue.edu/extmedia/FS/FS-18-W.pdf

Iowa

Like California, this state offers two levels for home-based food sellers. The first level allow you to sell foods that do not have to be refrigerated after production and these foods are referred to as non-potentially hazardous. Vendors can sell potentially hazardous foods—those that do need refrigeration and are perishable —with the second level certification.

Certifications: Non-potentially hazardous food vendors don't need anything to sell their products.

Potentially hazardous food vendors need a Home Food Establishment License and a kitchen inspection.

Maximum allowable income: No limitations

Approved venues: farmer's markets and home for those that sell non-potentially hazardous foods, and no restrictions on those that obtain a Home Food Establishment License.

For more information:
http://www.agmrc.org/media/cms/pm1294_f9a1b2 6af379b.pdf

Kansas

Certifications: None required.

Maximum allowable income: No limit.

Approved foods: non-potentially hazardous foods such as baked goods, fruit pies, fresh fruits and vegetables, nuts, and honey.

Approved venues: farmer's markets and events

For more information:
https://agriculture.ks.gov/divisions-programs/food-safety-lodging/food-sales-at-farmers'-markets

While Kansas doesn't have an official cottage food law, it does allow the above listed foods to be sold at farmer's markets and other events. To follow the Kansas Food Initiative, go here:
https://www.facebook.com/kansansforcottagefoods.

Kentucky

Although the state has no cottage food laws, they do offer a program for Homebased food processors, and I'll include the facts of that below.

Certifications: none required, but vendor must register each year with the Kentucky Cabinet for Health and Family Services/Food Safety Branch.

Maximum allowable income: No limit

Approved foods: fruit jams and jellies, syrups, fruit butters, baked goods, prepackaged mixed greens or herbs, dried fruits, vegetables, nuts, and herbs. In order to qualify for this program, "the final product must contain a primary or predominant ingredient which is a fruit, vegetable, nut or herb that is grown by a farmer in Kentucky."

Approved venues: farmer's markets, roadside stands, and farms.

For more information:
https://fcs-hes.ca.uky.edu/homebased_processing_microprocessing

Louisiana

Certifications: None, but the law requires very specific environmental regulations. (See link below)

Maximum allowable income: $20,000

Approved foods: baked goods to include breads, cakes, cookies, and pies, candies, dried mixes, honey and honeycomb products, jams, jellies, preserves, pickles and acidified foods, sauces, syrups, and spices.

Approved venues: farmer's markets, roadside stands, home, online, restaurants and stores (Please note that sellers of baked goods are not allowed to sell to restauarants and stores.)

For more information: http://www.rustonfarmersmarket.org/uploads/2/7/3/1/27317865/cottage_food_guidelines_hb_1270_simplified.pdf

Maine

Certification: registration and license required. A kitchen inspection is also required.

Maximum allowable income: No limit.

Approved foods: Baked goods, candies, fruit based jams and jellies, confections and any other food that does not require refrigeration. If you sell acid based foods such as pickles, salsas, marinades, dressings, and desert sauces like caramel or chocolate sauce, you are required to have them tested before you sell them.

Approved venues: Food sellers can sell at any venue.

For more information: https://extension.umaine.edu/publications/3101e/

Maryland

Certification: None required

Maximum allowable income: $25,000

Approved foods: breads, candies, non-flavored honey, pastries, pies, jams, jellies, chocolate covered items, granola, crackers, and pretzels.

Approved venues: Farmer's markets and special events

For more information:
http://mlis.state.md.us/2012rs/bills/sb/sb0550t.pdf

Massachusetts

Certification: Must get a permit and kitchen inspection. Some areas of the state require food safety training.

Maximum allowable income: No limit

Approved foods: breads, candies, pastries, jams, jellies, carmel corn, chocolate covered items, crackers, pretzels, granola, popcorn, nuts, and seeds.

Approved venues: farmer's markets, events, roadside stands, online, restaurants, stores, distributors, home

For more information:
http://www.mass.gov/eea/agencies/agr/markets/cul inary-tourism/massachusetts-food-processors-resource-manual-generic.html#chapter 9

Michigan

Certification: None required

Maximum allowable income: $20,000

Approved foods: breads, baked goods, pastries, jams, jellies, plain and flavored vinegar, dry herbs and mixtures, dry baking mixes, dry dips, dry soup, popcorn, cotton candy, coated or uncoated nuts, dried pasta, coffee, and chocolate covered items.

Approved venues: farmer's markets, home, roadside stands, events

For more information:
http://www.michigan.gov/mdard/0,4610,7-125-50772_45851-240577--,00.html

Minnesota

Certification: must register and take a food safety course

Maximum allowable income: $18,0000

Approved foods: non-potentially hazardous foods such as baked goods, jams, jellies, pickles, vegetables, and fruits. (All canned goods must have a PH of 4.6 or lower.)

Approved venues: farmer's markets, community events, home, online

For more information:
http://www.mda.state.mn.us/licensing/licensetypes/cottagefood.aspx

Note: Only the cottage food owner is allowed to deliver products to customers.

Mississippi

Certification: None required

Maximum allowable income: $20,000

Approved foods: baked goods, candy, chocolate covered nonperishable foods, dried fruit, dried pasta, dried spices, dry baking mixes, granola, cereal, trail mixes, dry rubs, and fruit pies.

Approved venues: farmer's markets, roadside stands, home, events

For more information:
http://msdh.ms.gov/msdhsite/_static/resources/5375.pdf

Missouri

Certification: None required

Maximum allowable income: $50,000

Approved foods: Baked goods, dried herbs, jams, and jellies

Approved venues: Farmer's markets, roadside stands, home, events

For more information:
http://www.house.mo.gov/billtracking/bills121/billpdf/intro/HB1508I.PDF

Montana

Certifications: None needed if only selling at farmer's market. For all other venues, sellers should register with their local health department.

Maximum allowable income: No limit

Approved foods: Breads, baked goods, pastries, crackers, cereals, granola, trail mix, nuts, snack mixes, jams, jellies, dried herbs, seasonings, and soups, honey, popcorn, popcorn balls, cotton candy, and candies.

Approved venues: Farmer's markets, roadside stands, home, events

For more information:
http://dphhs.mt.gov/publichealth/FCSS/cottagefood

Nebraska

Certifications: None required for cottage good vendors unless they sell at farmer's markets. A second type certification is allowed—a Home Food Establishment license—and it permits sellers to sell at any venue.

Maximum allowable income: No limit for cottage food producers, and $20,000 limit for Home Food Establishment vendors.

Approved foods: Breads, baked candies, pastries, granola, crackers, and pretzels.

Approved venues: All venues allowed for Home Food Establishment vendors, and cottage food venders can sell from home, or farmer's markets with a special permit.

For more information:
http://www.nda.nebraska.gov/publications/foods/food_safety_farmers_markets.pdf

Nevada

Certifications: must register with local health department in the area you're selling in.

Maximum allowable income: $35,000

Approved foods: Non-hazardous baked goods, nuts, nut mixes, candies, jams, jellies, preserves, plain and flavored vinegar, dry herbs, seasonings, dried fruits, cereal, trail mixes, granola, popcorn, and popcorn balls.

Approved venues: Farmer's markets, home, roadside stands, and events.

For more information:
https://legiscan.com/NV/text/SB206/id/850821

New Hampshire

Certifications: None required for cottage food vendors. If you exceed the income level or want to sell in other venues, you can get a Homestead License. See below link for more information on that level.

Maximum allowable income: $20,000

Approved foods: Breads, rolls, muffins, cookies, brownies, double crusted fruit pies, candies, fudge, packaged dry goods, jams, and jellies.

Approved venues: farmer's markets, home, farm stands, retail store

For more information:
http://www.dhhs.nh.gov/dphs/fp/sanitation/homestead.htm

New Jersey

This state does not offer cottage food laws. For more information on the efforts being conducted to pass a law, see this website:
http://www.njhomebakersbill.org/

New Mexico

Certifications: This state requires cottage food vendors to submit an extensive application, have a kitchen inspection, and take a free training course. Unfortunately, residents of Albuquerque cannot sell food made from home.

Maximum allowable income: No limit

Approved foods: jams and jellies that contain high sugar, non-cream filled baked goods, tortillas, candies, fudge, and dry mixes that are made with commercially processed ingredients.

Approved venues: Farmer's markets, fiestas and roadside stands.

For more information:
https://www.env.nm.gov/fod/Food_Program/HomeBasedProcessing.htm

New York

Certifications: Must register, and the state has the right to inspect your kitchen at any time.

Maximum allowable income: No limit

Approved foods: Baked goods, jams, jellies, marmalades, dried spices or herbs made with commercially produced products, popcorn, caramel corn, peanut brittle, candies, excluding chocolate.

Approved venues: Farmer's markets, farm stands, and events that are agriculturally based.

For more information:
http://www.agriculture.ny.gov/FS/consumer/processor.html

North Carolina

Certifications: Vendors must submit an extensive application and then have their kitchen inspection. The state allows no pets in the home—not even temporarily.

Maximum allowable income: No limit

Approved foods: Baked goods, jams, jellies, candies, dried spices, some sauces and liquids, pickles and other acidified foods.

Approved venues: Vendors can sell at any location.

For more information:
http://www.ncagr.gov/fooddrug/food/homebiz.htm

North Dakota

This state doesn't have cottage food laws, but vendors are allowed to sell homemade food products.

Certifications: None required.

Maximum allowable income: No limit

Approved foods: baked goods and canned goods, but restrictions vary by county, so check with yours.

Approved venues: Farmer's markets, roadside stands, certain community events.

For more information:
Since laws vary by county, you should contact your county health department.

Ohio

Certifications: No requirements for cottage food producers. Home bakeries are allowed and must be certified.

Maximum allowable income: No limit.

Approved foods: baked goods, candies, jams, jellies, fruit butters, granola, popcorn, unfilled baked donuts, waffle cones, caramel corn, pizzelles, dry cereal, nut snack mixes, seasonings, roasted coffee, dry baking mixes, dry herbs and blends, rubs, and tea blends.

Approved venues: farmer's markets, events, home, restaurants, grocery stores, online

For more information:
http://www.agri.ohio.gov/foodsafety/food-cottageindex.htm

Oklahoma

Certifications: None required

Maximum allowable income: $20,000

Approved foods: Baked goods that don't contain meat or fruit

Approved venues: Sellers can only sell from their homes

For more information:
http://webserver1.lsb.state.ok.us/cf_pdf/2013-14%20ENR/hB/HB1094%20ENR.PDF

Oregon

Certifications: food handler's license

Maximum allowable income: $20,000

Approved foods: Breads, candies, honey, pastries, candied apples, chocolate covered items, crackers, pretzels, marshmallows, and granola

Approved venues: Farmer's markets, events, home, roadside stands

For more information:
https://www.oregon.gov/ODA/programs/FoodSafety/FSLicensing/Pages/DomesticKitchen.aspx

Pennsylvania

Certifications: Must register and renew the license annually. Also, the state requires testing for certain types of products.

Maximum allowable income: No limit.

Approved foods: Food that are not "time and temperature controlled for safety." In other words, foods that don't require refrigeration or that are perishable.

Approved venues: Producers can sell anywhere.

For more information:
http://www.agriculture.pa.gov/Protect/FoodSafety/
Processing%20Wholesale%20and%20Distribution/
Pages/Limited-Food-Establishment-.aspx#.Vn6yrrx2rdk

Rhode Island

Rhode Island does not have cottage food laws and only permits farmers who sell at least $2,500 per year of agricultural products to produce food from homes and sell to the general public.

For more information about the farmer's program, go here: http://www.dem.ri.gov/programs/bnatres/
agricult/pdf/farmhome.pdf

South Carolina

Certifications: None required, but producers are required to get a business license for tax purposes.

Maximum allowable income: $15,000

Approved foods: baked goods and candy

Approved venues: Farmer's markets, roadside stands, home, and events

For more information:
https://agriculture.sc.gov/wp-content/uploads/
2014/09/Cottage-Food-FAQ-Angie2.pdf

South Dakota

Certifications: No permit needed, but most foods must be tested and certificate displayed when selling them.

Maximum allowable income: No limit

Approved foods: Baked goods, candies, and canned goods.

Approved venues: Farmer's markets, roadside stands, events, and online, but customers must pick up orders.

For more information:
http://www.dakotarural.org/eat-local-foods/home-processed-foods-law/

Tennessee

Certifications: Cottage food producers are encourage to get a permit and kitchen inspection, but it's not required. However, if you want to sell wholesale to restaurants and stores, you must get a domestic kitchen license.

Maximum allowable income: No limit for cottage food producers, but domestic kitchen producers are limited to 100 units per week. Also, no pets are allowed.

Approved foods: Cottage food producers can only sell non-potentially hazardous products such as jams, jellies, and dried mixes, while domestic kitchen producers can also sell potentially hazardous products, including baked products that contain eggs.

Approved venues: Farmer's markets, roadside stands, home, events, and online. Domestic kitchen producers can also sell to restaurants and stores. Neither type of producer can cater, and that includes delivering custom cakes.

For more information:
https://ag.tennessee.edu/foodscience/Documents/
Getting%20Started%20in%20a%20Food%20Manufa
cturing%20Business%20in%20Tennessee.pdf and
https://ag.tennessee.edu/cpa/Information%20Sheets
/CPA%20194.pdf

Texas

Certifications: None required, but must take a food safety education course.

Maximum allowable income: $50,000

Approved foods: Baked goods, candies, coated and uncoated nuts, unroasted nut butters, jams, jellies, fruit pies, dehydrated fruits or vegetables (including dried beans), popcorn, popcorn snacks, cereal, granola, dry mises, vinegars, pickles, mustard, roasted coffee, dry tea, dried herbs or mixes.

Approved venues: Farmer's markets, events, roadside stands, home

For more information:
http://www.dshs.texas.gov/foodestablishments/
cottagefood/default.aspx

Utah

Certifications: This state requires a business license, food safety training, a kitchen inspection, and for the vendor to submit recipes and samples for all of their products.

Maximum allowable income: No limit

Approved foods: Breads, candies, sauces, vinegars, dry goods such as cereals, granola, herbs, spices and seasonings, whole hardboiled eggs, pastries, jams, jellies, marmalades and other preserves, popcorn, caramel corn, granola, marshmallows, chocolate covered items, crackers, pretzels, nuts, and seeds. Vendors are not allowed to sell fermented foods or pickles.

Approved venues: Vendors can sell anywhere in the state of Utah. The only exception is that restaurants my not use your products as an ingredient in the food they sell.

For more information:
http://ag.utah.gov/cottage-food-production.html

Vermont

Certifications: Vendors who sell less than $125 per week in baked goods don't need permits, registration or inspections, but if you exceed that, you need a Home Bakery License, which requires a license and kitchen inspection.

Maximum allowable income: No limit

Approved foods: Low risk baked goods

Approved venues: Farmer's markets, roadside stands, home, events, online

For more information:
http://dec.vermont.gov/sites/dec/files/permit-handbook/sheetHCbake.pdf

Virginia

Certifications: There is a lengthy process to get set up that includes an application, permits, training, and a kitchen inspection.

Maximum allowable income: No limit.

Approved foods: You can forego the inspection is you product only these foods: candies, baked goods, and jams and jellies. To sell any other type of food, you must go through the application process.

Approved venues: Without an inspection, you can sell at farmer's markets and home. For all other venues including roadside stands, online, events, restaurants, and stores, you must have an inspection. (Only catering is not approved—you must have a commercial license for this.)

For more information:
http://loudounfarmersmarkets.org/apply/vdacs-resources-information/

Washington

Certifications: The state requires an expensive and drawn out process. Vendors must first take a training course, get a business license, submit an application that includes a detailed business plan and recipes, which will have to be approved, and then get their kitchen inspected.

Maximum allowable income: $25,000

Approved foods: Breads, baked goods, candies, vinegar, pastries, jams, jellies and other preserves, crackers, pretzels, granola, nuts, seeds, cereals, coffee, tea, herbs, spices, and seasonings, fried donuts, tortillas, pizzelles, krumkake, potato chips, kale chips and other items like them, stove top candies such as peanut brittle, fudge, and taffy, products dipped or coated in chocolate, molded chocolates.

Approved venues: Farmer's markets, online (cannot be shipped, but delivered or picked up), home, events, and roadside stands.

For more information:
http://agr.wa.gov/FoodAnimal/CottageFoodOperation

West Virginia

Certifications: The state recommends that you contact your local health department because each county is different.

Maximum allowable income: No limit

Approved foods: Non-potentially hazardous baked goods and candies, apple butter, sorghum, molasses, jams, jellies,

Approved venues: Farmer's markets

For more information:
http://smallfarmcenter.ext.wvu.edu/r/download/366 41 and
http://smallfarmcenter.ext.wvu.edu/farmers_markets /vendors_guide

Wisconsin

Certifications: The state encourages training, but does not require it.

Maximum allowable income: $5,000

Approved foods: Jams, jellies, pickled sauces, and any other canned good that has a PH of 4.6 or lower, sauerkraut, fresh fruits and vegetables, raw and pasteurized cider, honey, maple syrup, popcorn.

Approved venues: Farmer's markets and events.

For more information: There is a current lawsuit brought by three woman who are asking the state to improve their cottage food laws and allow home cooks to sell baked goods. You can read about it here: http://ij.org/case/wisconsin-baked-good-ban/

Wyoming

Certifications: None required

Maximum allowable income: No limit

Approved foods: Vendors can sell ANY type of food as long as it doesn't have any meat (other than poultry) in it. This is the most lax cottage food law in the country.

Approved venues: Vendors can sell anywhere except they cannot sell their goods wholesale to restaurants or stores. In addition, if they are sold online, they must be picked up or delivered in person. Finally, the one quirk in the law says that the goods must be eaten in a private home, so no catering, or cakes for functions outside of a home (including weddings.)

For more information: http://legisweb.state.wy.us/2015/Enroll/HB0056.pdf

Again, if a law has changed and I haven't caught it, please email me at samkernsbooks@gmail.com and I'll make the correction in the book immediately!

Conclusion

Well, that was fun, wasn't it? There's nothing like taking a look at your dreams and then learning the practical steps necessary to make them a reality. I sincerely hope that's what this book has done for you. Not only can I tell you from experience that running a food business is a great way to make a living, but it's also one of the most rewarding ways you can spend your time.

If my book has been helpful to you, will you consider leaving a review for it on Amazon? Good reviews always help people decide whether or not they should purchase a book, and to be honest, it helps the authors further their careers.

I wish you the best in your food endeavors, and remember to contact me with any questions or concerns at samkernsbooks@gmail.com.

Thanks to you,
Sam

Thank you for buying

How to Start a Home-Based Food Business:
Turn Your Foodie Love into Serious Cash
with a Food Business Startup
(The Work from Home Series: Book 3)

Sign up at my website RainMakerPress.com for
special offers, promotions, and information about
new releases in this series.